REMARKABLE WOMEN
OF THE SECOND WORLD WAR

REMARKABLE WOMEN
OF THE SECOND WORLD WAR
A Collection of Untold Stories

VICTORIA PANTON BACON

Cover illustration: Women of the ATS during the Second World War, Alamy/Mirrorpix.
Author photo: Simone Sisterson.

First published 2022

The History Press
97 St George's Place, Cheltenham,
Gloucestershire, GL50 3QB
www.thehistorypress.co.uk

British Library Cataloguing in Publication Data.
A catalogue record for this book is available from the British Library.

ISBN 978 0 7509 9996 0

Typesetting and origination by The History Press
Printed and bound in Great Britain by TJ Books Limited, Padstow, Cornwall.

Trees for LYfe

CONTENTS

FOREWORD

BY THE HON CAPTAIN
RT HON PENNY MORDAUNT MP

Any history, no matter how well written, can never fully illuminate what people experienced. Unlike the protagonists, the reader already knows how things will end. We cannot help but view the action with that comfort in mind. We can only imagine the anguish and uncertainty for those who lived during this major conflict.

That is why personal stories matter. They get us closer to what people actually experienced. Closer to what it took to endure. To understand how hope was kept alive. How their lives were changed. For women that change was profound.

That is why this book is such a valuable contribution to our knowledge of this period. The stories it contains are about real people. Victoria gives us a glimpse into the world of a woman or young girl and 'their war', be they a nurse, evacuee, engineer, pilot, mother or child. This book is essential reading for anyone with an unsatiable curiosity about the Second World War.

However, these precious testimonies reveal lessons that go beyond that moment. *Remarkable Women of the Second World War* teaches us about humanity. Suffering and turmoil was intense and inescapable. That is why these true stories, honestly told and honestly written, are so important – we can gather strength from the strength of these women, courage from their courage, and believe in humanity, as they believed.

The book is also timely. Our own recent experiences of the pandemic can give us perhaps more empathy with life and death situations, the national effort, and emotional and practical sacrifice.

Victoria writes of her care for the women whose stories she has told in her introduction, a care which resonates throughout the whole of this book. They take us through the full spectrum of human emotions: the drama, death and destruction but also the joy, beauty and humour. The spirit of Vera Saies, our Battle of Britain plotter, who broke WAAF rules on an evening out to wear bright red lipstick; the comfort Dorothy Drew, our homesick child evacuee, gained from feeding kittens warm milk at the farm she was sent to during the Blitz; the amusement Gwen Raggett, our Land Girl, found in hiding from Italian prisoners-of-war who pestered her with love songs; and the sticky buns Midori Yamazaki, our Japanese teenager, spoke of that made her exhausting factory work more bearable.

Victoria was determined from the moment she began planning this remarkable book to reflect the fact the Second World War was a truly global conflict. Amongst the British memories there are recollections from former Yugoslavia, Russia, Burma, Japan and two stories of European Jews who were young girls when the Nazis devastated their family lives.

There is still a paucity of work which tell the stories of half the population at these key moments in our national history. Victoria has done us a huge service in this unique, varied, and vital collection of tales.

In reading it, when we are facing our own challenges, when we do not yet know how they will end, we can draw from these stories and all they have to teach. It is a book of Remembrance. It is a book about hope.

The Hon Captain Rt Hon Penny Mordaunt MP
Royal Navy Reserve
MP for Portsmouth North

INTRODUCTION

BY VICTORIA PANTON BACON

I am very pleased to have reached the stage of writing the introduction to this book. Learning about the wartime lives of every one of the *Remarkable Women* whose stories are revealed on its pages has been eminently rewarding, truly fascinating – and in every way, a privilege.

These are their stories, based on truthful memories shared with me. Every chapter, however, tells the story of so many women who lived through the Second World War as they did. Because of the honesty of these women so many more can be remembered; the revelations on these pages not only deepen our knowledge of the lives of so many women, but our understanding too.

We can, and must, learn from these remarkable women and draw strength from the many examples of courage, resilience, and determination that scatter the pages of this book. These women – all of them very young during the war, of course, and some were children – experienced so much: separation from families, grief, fear of being killed, physical pain. And there was nothing to protect them from the reality that humankind could be very cruel. Many were, admittedly, scarred forever by their wartime circumstances, and shaped by them, but all of them continued to show remarkable courage as they picked up the pieces of their shattered lives in the post-war years, too.

The Second World War was a global conflict; I have done my best to reflect this fact with these stories. In addition to six British chapters, there are memories given to me by women from the Netherlands, Germany, Burma, Russia, Croatia, and Japan. These stories – and the British chapters which include, amongst others, a Women's Land Army memory, an RAF nurse's story, and a child evacuee account – will reveal much that is surprising, poignant, intriguing – and *remarkable*.

There will be much about these women you will admire, too; I have done them a disservice if you do not. As each chapter has unfolded, whilst piecing together the individual stories, I have grown to respect and care so much for all of them. My greatest wish would be that they were all still alive today and we could all be together in a lovely warm room, drinking tea and feeling happy, safe, and fascinated in each other's company.

That can't happen, of course, but you can read their stories; you can let them into your lives through their words, as I have done.

You will be enriched by their recollections; of this, I am certain.

Victoria Panton Bacon

PART 1

THE BRITISH MEMORIES

DOROTHY DREW:
A CHILD EVACUEE

Backwards, forwards, backwards, forwards … enjoying the sunshine and the motion of the small wooden swing she was propelling with her 7½-year-old legs, Dorothy Drew was feeling as happy as could be in the garden of 89 Parkside Avenue, in Romford, on the morning of 3 September 1939. Dorothy loved her swing – it was hers and hers alone because she didn't have brothers or sisters to share it. She loved its gentle movement, listening to the birds as she swung, thinking only of what she might be having for lunch, or even about what she had had for breakfast.

Then her father came into the garden and held the swing so all forward – and backward – movement stopped. She told me she jumped off the swing, and said:

> I remember my father ushering me quickly into the kitchen, where mother was waiting, looking anxious. 'We have to listen to the radio,' father said, 'we have to listen to Mr Chamberlain on the wireless, because what he is going to say is very important.'

The radio was in the kitchen of their small house in Romford, in the East End of London. Her mother was very fond of the house and the kitchen was her favourite room. Her father (an electrical engineer) devoted as much time as he could to his gadgets, making and fixing whatever he could; he was as practical as he was thrifty. He was, Dorothy told me, particularly proud of this wireless set, which he had made himself. She said: 'It was a great big set, that sat in an alcove in the corner of the room, with enormous valves on it.' Quite often, as a child, Dorothy had 'watched' the radio whilst people talked, imagining the faces behind the voices.

However, there was no childish fun to be had in Mr Chamberlain's words that emanated from her father's wireless that morning. Confirming that Britain had declared war with Germany, because Germany had refused to withdraw its troops from Poland, Prime Minister Neville Chamberlain said:

I am speaking to you from the Cabinet Room at 10 Downing Street. This morning the British ambassador in Berlin handed the German government a final note stating that unless we heard from them by 11 o'clock that they were prepared at once to withdraw their troops from Poland, a state of war would exist between us. I have to tell you now that no such undertaking has been received, and that consequently this country is at war with Germany.

You can imagine what a bitter blow it is to me that all my long struggle to win peace has failed. Yet I cannot believe that there is anything more, or anything different, that I could have done and that would have been more successful. Up to the very last it would have been quite possible to have arranged a peaceful and honourable settlement between Germany and Poland. But Hitler would not have it. He had evidently made up his mind to attack Poland whatever happened, and although he now says he put forward reasonable proposals which were rejected by the Poles, that is not a true statement. The proposals were never shown to the Poles, nor to us, and though they were announced in the German broadcast on Thursday night, Hitler did not wait to hear comments on them, but ordered his troops to cross the Polish frontier the next morning.

His action shows convincingly that there is no chance of expecting that this man will ever give up his practice of using force to gain his will. He can only be stopped by force.

We have a clear conscience. We have done all that any country could do to establish peace. But the situation in which no word given by Germany's ruler could be trusted, and no people or country could feel itself safe, had become intolerable. And now that we have resolved to finish it, I know that you will all play your part with calmness and courage.

'It wasn't a huge surprise,' Dorothy recalled:

I think everybody knew that the Prime Minister was going to declare we would be going to war with Germany, but we didn't know when. After

Mr Chamberlain spoke my father, who was very good at explaining things, told me why the war was inevitable; Mr Chamberlain had been left with no choice but to make the decision he did because of Germany invading Poland, making life so difficult for the Poles.

Her father's words of explanation may have been to reassure Dorothy, as much as he felt able, that there was reason in what was happening. But as much as he would have wanted to reassure his daughter, how could he? How could anyone be reassuring on such a day? The only certainty of war was uncertainty; but even the extent and nature of uncertainty was unclear. How long would it last? Who would have to go and fight? Would their small family be broken up? Would they still have enough food? Questions, questions, questions asked by the millions in the United Kingdom and in Europe whose lives were instantly altered with the announcement that the Second World War had begun. Questions for which there were no answers, no option left but for all – whatever their situation – to adhere to Mr Chamberlain's instruction, to 'play [your] part with calmness and courage'.

After Dorothy told me how she received the news that their lives were about to become very different, I could not help but think of my own childhood – and about children I know today that are of the age that Dorothy was when she heard this. The years between being a toddler and a teenager are widely understood to be 'formative' years, when we learn to read, to count, to ride a bicycle perhaps – to constantly learn, without knowing that we are little sponges, absorbing, absorbing, absorbing. I remember from my childhood this was the time I would walk in woods with my father and learn the names of trees, birds and butterflies. We don't know how precious our childhood is until it has passed, until those carefree days are replaced by adulthood – possessed of course of its own joys but accompanied by duties and responsibilities that don't go away. Dorothy's story therefore reveals another consequence of war that I hadn't thought about so much before, until she opened my mind to it: the fact that quite simply, thousands of children were robbed of the sweetness of childhood. When I was that age I might have known a bit about war, but I had no understanding at all about the fact that human beings could be so cruel. I am sure I didn't appreciate that one human being would ever want to kill another.

Dorothy outside her
Romford home, c. 1938.

Dorothy on her swing.

As the Second World War began to unfold in the days, weeks, and months that followed Prime Minister Chamberlain's announcement, the way that life changed for children, inevitably, varied immeasurably depending upon their age and situation. Thousands of children – Dorothy's age but younger and older too – would have had to get used to a home that was suddenly without the presence of a father or brother. Mothers left behind would have been weighed down with extra duty and care, leaning on their young ones for practical, and even emotional support. School must have been a very different experience too; children in village schools suddenly 'invaded' by youngsters from towns who came to them as evacuees – so class sizes suddenly bulged and children, as different as chalk and cheese, had to learn to accept each other. Thousands of children, too, discovered the pain of bereavement, and loss – homes taken away, as well as so many loved ones.

That said, amongst the loneliness, extra responsibility, new-found fears (and food rationing), aspects of war did, for some youngsters, prove to be exciting. How many would not have been thrilled by the sight of one, or often more, aircraft tearing across the sky; enormous, roaring machines, sometimes even dropping men with parachutes? There are also tales of the excitement children felt when 'pillaging' parts off fallen enemy aircraft – anything they could grab including levers and switches from cockpits, bits of propellers, lights and wheel nuts. And, of course, child evacuation – from the city to the country – had some delightful consequences too. For the first time, thousands of city children were able, for example, to run freely in country lanes, see spring lambs, bluebells and mountains, and even swim in the sea. There are also many heartening stories of lasting friendships that formed as the contrasting worlds of city and country children came together.

However, I will return now to Dorothy – this is her story. The story of a little girl whose Second World War began when she was 7½, and ended when she was 13. You will recall she was in the comfort of her parent's kitchen as the Second World War began. Nothing much happened for the first few days, but then, for Dorothy, it became inescapably real:

A lady appeared at the house, a week or so after the war began. She told my parents I would have to be evacuated, because Romford – where we lived – was near the docks, so it was deemed a high-risk area and too dangerous for me to stay there. I didn't want to go and didn't really understand either why I had to because we hadn't been bombed or anything by that point. My mother didn't want me to go, she was really sad, but the decision had been taken anyway. I remember feeling very disappointed because I loved my school too, it was called Havering Road School. But the next thing I recall was being put on a coach, I thought my mother was coming with me, but she didn't. I was one of lots of children put on this coach, which was taking us to a place called Layer Marney in Essex. It was just a village then …

I don't remember details after that, such as a getting off the coach, or being collected by anyone, my memory is rather hazy … but I can recall crying whilst we were driving along, and most of the other children crying too. However, I do recall the little farmhouse I was taken to with about five of the other children; and the lady who took us in, who was in her 30s, being very kind. She showed us their animals: lambs, kittens, chickens … I remember thinking how lovely they were. I recall having to share a big bed with a little girl who was about the same age as me, who wet this bed because she was so nervous. I used to get up during the night sometimes and stare out of the window, wondering which was the way home; I desperately wanted to go home, I was so home sick.

I was there, I think, for about eight weeks – as were all the other children. It wasn't horrid, I was just homesick. We used to have a meal at midday, the food was mostly alright but almost every day we had cabbage and I hated cabbage so when no one was looking, I would scrape it off the plate and hide it underneath it. Silly what you remember! I did get told off, but not really punished, and as I said the lady whose house it was, I forget her name, was very kind, especially to me, because she let me feed the kittens every day. I think it was because I was more homesick than the others, there were a couple of boys in the house who didn't seem to mind being away from home too much. Anyway, back to the kittens. The kind lady had a great big old-fashioned Yorkshire pudding pan in the yard, and after the cows were milked I was allowed to put some of the fresh milk into this pan and give it to the kittens, who would paddle in it as well as drink it; feeding and playing with the kittens was the highlight of being there for me. I did this every morning. Then, finally, by about the end October, we were all allowed to go home.

Dorothy told me she couldn't have been happier when she was told she was allowed to go home. But she said that when she got back, everything felt different. She said, 'Bombing had already begun. My parents were so anxious all the time.' She explained that her father had not been called up for service because he would have failed his medical, as he had had rheumatic fever as a child. However, he would also have been excused from service as he worked as an electrical inspector, which counted as a 'reserved occupation', i.e. someone working in a vital role that helped to keep the country going. Other reserved occupations included doctors, farmers, teachers, miners, and shopkeepers:

> Of course, I was very glad my father hadn't had to go away, but my mother and I still worried about him when he went to work. He went off each day on a motorbike, with a sidecar (which I'd sit in sometimes; that was fun!) because we wouldn't have been able to afford the petrol for a car. He looked so vulnerable going off in that little motor – the smallest bit of 'ack ack' would have got him.
>
> I remember a couple of very 'close shaves' my father had – one day he came from work with the bottom of one his trouser legs ripped off, after an incendiary bomb had dropped very near him, causing it to catch fire; and another time he was in our garden having a smoke, and a piece of shrapnel shot past him and landed a few feet away, with such ferocity it pierced the concrete next to him.

Soon after her return home from Layer Marney, Dorothy went to her garden to play and was upset to see an Anderson shelter[1]; it wasn't so much that this shelter was there – by this time war had made its presence felt and knowing there was a place of safety would probably have been a relief – but it was the fact that the shelter had been put up in place of their garden rockery, of which she had been so fond. She told me how her father had built this rockery himself and she loved it. The loss of something like a garden rockery during the war when so much was lost – entire buildings, aircraft and, of course, most importantly, people – might seem irrelevant, even crass to mention, but I think it matters, especially for this Second World War memory. For a child to lose something like this feels very poignant: a symbol of the change all around her around her, none of which she – or more importantly her parents – could have any control of at all. Yet another part of Dorothy's childhood taken away, never to come back, because of the war.

Dorothy told me about how they shared this shelter with the family next door; it was the norm for shelters to be shared between two families. It was a government-supplied standard issue Anderson shelter, so, like all shelters at the beginning of the war (as it progressed larger ones were made that could accommodate more people) it was around 6½ft by 4½ft – therefore, small and a squash even for the smallest families. Dorothy said:

> I had a 'siren suit'[2] by my bed in our house, which I had to quickly put on if we heard the screaming of the air-raid siren and had to go to the shelter in the middle of the night. This was a special suit, a bit like a onesie, which kept me warm. I think my parents slept in their clothes, to save dressing time. If it was night-time I would try to sleep in the shelter, but it was always difficult and uncomfortable because I had to share a small bunk bed with the boy from next door, he was called Kenny, and was about my age. We went 'head-to-toe', it was very uncomfortable, and he had horribly smelly feet!

Their homes were also very near an 'ack ack' gun position, from where soldiers would repeatedly shoot at enemy aircraft during raids, which was, inevitably, very noisy.

But most of all Dorothy remembered how frightened she felt when they were in the shelter. Sometimes the two families would simply be there, together, silently listening to the fearful noise of the bombing going on above them. The shelters were – amazingly – pretty much bombproof, but were nonetheless very cramped, draughty and would have been cold and damp, especially if it had been raining. Also, once in the shelter, they didn't know how long they would have to stay there. Dorothy told me they learnt to distinguish between the sound of German and British aircraft: 'Ours,' said Dorothy, 'seemed to move across the sky, making a continuous humming sound, whereas the German planes went 'zum, zum, zum …'' She told me she has not forgotten, to this day, the fear she felt sitting in this shelter – so much so that she is still, eighty years later, troubled and afraid when subjected to unexpected, loud, inexplicable noises.

Rushing into air-raid shelters after the 'scream' of an order to do so became a feature of her life back at Havering Road school, too. These shelters, of course, were much larger – around 40ft long. Dorothy recalled how the teachers would hurry the children into the shelter, doing their best to keep them calm, giving them water and biscuits. The only light they had in the shelters, which were otherwise dingy and dark, was from candles, the small flames providing an immensely comforting glow. But what strange times, especially for a child. They had to get used to gas masks too – always having one about their person, when they weren't having to wear them. Dorothy told me:

> Lots of children found these really tricky and uncomfortable, including me because I was a bit claustrophobic. Very young children, toddlers really, were given masks that looked a bit like Mickey Mouse – with Mickey's nose and ears. I had one of these at the beginning, which did help me get used to a bigger one.

The extraordinary strength of the shelters was laid to bare for Dorothy one day at school when she was in the shelter, with her friends and teachers of course, and above them they heard the sound of some of their school buildings taking a direct hit; the resulting damage so severe their school was closed. This bombing occurred during the Blitz – a strategic bombing campaign unleashed by the Germans over a number of cities and towns in the United Kingdom, which began towards the end of the Battle of Britain (September 1940), continuing until May 1941. The term 'Blitz' was first used by the British press – it means 'lightning' – and originated from the term 'Blitzkrieg', which is the German word for 'lightning war'.

Another moment of paralysing fear she recalled occurred one day, towards the end of 1940, when Dorothy and her mother were queuing up at a local market for their weekly share of whale meat, which was the only meat available to them at the time: 'we certainly wouldn't have chosen it,' she said. 'It was really fatty, disgusting and tasted how you might expect rotten fish to taste.' They were two of around fifty people lining up for their ration, when suddenly they were all 'strafed' from above by a German aircraft that flew low over them, dropping bullets. Dorothy described how her mother pushed her very quickly to the ground and lay on top of her; everyone was doing the same thing. After a while, when silence replaced the noise of the aircraft, the people gradually began to look up from their horizontal positions and bravely, slowly, took their places in the queue.

It was while the Blitz was well under way, at the beginning of 1941, that Dorothy – once again – was sent away; it was, quite simply, too dangerous for her to stay in London. She went, on this occasion, to Alconbury in Cambridgeshire, to stay with her maternal grandmother. However, knowing no other children and being without her parents too, this was a lonely and troubling time for her. She told me she struggled to settle there and how unhappy she was at her new school too. She recalled:

> I was a fish out of water. I didn't like this new school, especially at the beginning. I only had my school uniform to wear from my old school – a brown blazer and a brown skirt – and the other children teased me because they didn't have any sort of uniform. They teased me about the way I spoke too. It was horrible.
>
> But my grandmother (Grandma Townsend) more than made up for it. It was only her and me in the house because my grandfather had died before I was born. She looked after me wonderfully – I slept on beautifully ironed cotton sheets, and I often woke to the smell of delicious sausages, or bacon. I think my grandmother was quite friendly with the local butcher, because I am sure we had more than our fair share of meat!
>
> One of my grandmother's favourite things was her piano – she couldn't read music but she was able to play a tune just from hearing it – and Sunday afternoons became very special because she would open the window and some of the American airmen, who arrived in Alconbury in the summer of 1942, would gather round and say 'Grandma Townsend, play us a tune!' I remember her mostly playing the 'Missouri Waltz' (a Johnny Cash tune) and 'Camptown Races'.

However, soon after her arrival in Alconbury, Dorothy received the very sad news that her Romford home had been hit by an incendiary bomb and had been almost completely destroyed. Thankfully, her parents were not at home at the time so were physically unscathed, but the mental scarring it caused, particularly for her mother, never went away. 'My poor mother,' said Dorothy, 'it simply made her so depressed. She was never the same again.' Dorothy went on to tell me about a few of the belongings that her parents did manage to retrieve from the damage, including a small clock that had sat on a mantelpiece in the kitchen, which her mother loved and kept, despite it being charred. The only item of Dorothy's that was salvaged was a china 'bunny', with a peculiarly large, round nose. 'This bunny has watched over me ever since he was returned safely to me,' Dorothy said.

However – as every cloud has a silver lining – the bombing of the family home resulted in her parents joining her in Alconbury, which, despite the awfulness of losing her home, was a huge relief for Dorothy, still not even 10 years old:

> My father was given £750 from the War Commission – which of course sounds very little these days but was actually quite a lot then – after our house was bombed, which he eventually used to pay for the building of a bungalow. In the meantime, after he arrived in Alconbury, he got a job with the local Air Ministry doing I am not sure what but I think it was quite important! He also worked as an Auxiliary Firemen and spent a lot of time fishing.

There wasn't room at her grandmother's house for the three of them to stay very long, so they had to find other accommodation. Displacement such as this would have been a feature of life for so many families; to lose everything, in such frightening circumstances, is barely imaginable. Their 'rescue' came with an invitation to live in part of the Vicarage in Alconbury – the family there, Dorothy recalled, were kind and generously invited Dorothy and her parents to stay there as long as they needed. However, their living quarters were small attic rooms at the top of the house. Dorothy shared a bedroom with her parents – a room with two windows – but there was only one window in their kitchen/sitting-room and the dinginess of it Dorothy thinks, made her mother's depression worse.

'I don't blame my mother for finding it so difficult,' Dorothy said:

> She had lost so much; and she was very house-proud, she was the sort of person who liked everything to be very neat and tidy; which was virtually impossible in our tiny, rather dark attic. The washing was tricky too. But we were safe, and things did eventually start to look 'up' and get better. My father managed to buy 1½ acres of land, for about £80, enough to build on and began to design and build a new house for us, which was to be a lovely bungalow. But it took a long time … it wasn't easy to get materials, of course, during the war, and every bit of material had to be licensed too.

Dorothy recalled how as her parents began to plan their new home, she felt happier too, and with that school also became more bearable. At last, once again, Dorothy was able to sit in her classroom and concentrate on her schoolwork, without the interruption of an air-raid siren screaming. But, as with almost all children – wartime or not – it was the holidays children looked forward to more than anything. It was with much joy that she, and her friends, were told that if they were prepared to undertake some of the jobs that weren't being done because so many young men had been sent away, they would be 'richly rewarded' with extra holidays.

These were not 'unpleasant jobs' said Dorothy, who then described a cheerful 'children's army' – tripping over themselves to be as useful as possible. 'There were lots of different things for us to do,' she said:

> The boys did a lot of potato picking – they would walk behind horses pulling ploughs, collecting the potatoes that came to the surface. I – with other girls – would collect old newspapers from people in the town. We would take them into school; it was all very well organised – if you collected a few newspapers you would be given a badge saying 'Private'; if you managed to get a lot you would be a 'General' – we all wanted to be a 'General'! I was quite lucky, I became a 'General' quite quickly – my parents took the Daily Telegraph every day and the Vicar took The Times, so I didn't have to go very far even to get a few papers. The boys, too, were encouraged to catch rats. They were not allowed to bring a whole rat into school, but had to prove they'd caught a rat by bringing in the tails, and they'd get a penny for each one.

Helping harvest corn, in the autumns of 1942 and 1943, was also something many of the children enjoyed helping with. They would collect the corn (this was called gleaning) after it came out of the thrashing machines and stack it into pyramid-shaped 'stooks', the idea being that it would dry more quickly if it were in a (rough) pyramid shape for the farmer to bundle it up.

'It all sounds a bit crazy now,' Dorothy said, 'but actually these jobs were important and needed to be done. As children, we felt were taking part in the war effort.' At the same time, too, without realising it probably, they were learning vital lifelong lessons of responsibility and teamwork. Meanwhile, rationing of food and food shortages were commonplace for everyone, including in the countryside; and all who had some land were obliged, by the War Commission, to grow vegetables for distribution to those who needed them most. Dorothy's father, on his paddock, planted lots of potatoes; and later in the war she described quite a little farmholding developing; in addition to vegetables they had lots of hens, and a 'cycle' of having two pigs … resulting in inevitable slaughter, every few weeks, which Dorothy found very upsetting because she became very fond them.

In spite of her mother's despair about losing their Romford home, and the continuation of the war, this was not an entirely sad time. As Dorothy began to settle in Alconbury, she became good friends with the Vicar's niece, Valerie. She recalled the fun the two girls had together, dressing up, and selling roses and other flowers from the garden – keeping some of the pennies they made for themselves, but also giving some to charity. However, Dorothy did admit to quite a lot of naughtiness – including stealing food for midnight feasts and pretending to be ghosts adorned in sheets they would take from the large vicarage linen cupboard.

I should explain, too, that the airfield at Alconbury[3] had, by this time, become an important American airbase – the US 8th Army Air Force[4] arrived there in 1942, their fleet of B-24 Liberators replacing the earlier Royal Air Force Wellington bomber squadrons. In order to accommodate the Liberators – one of the largest of the American heavy bomber aircraft that had four engines and needed a crew of ten to function – runways had to be extended and extra hangars had to be built. Dorothy told me:

It was quite thrilling to watch these enormous American aircraft take off. We would count them as they would go in and out. But one day was awful. I remember one of the planes making a really strange noise. As it came in, towards the incline of a hill, it crashed, and was buried in the hillside. All the crew died. It was dreadful, some of the local people got on their bikes, out of curiosity, to get close to the bomb site.

Dorothy spoke fondly of the Americans, most of whom were jolly and very friendly, and more than happy to integrate with the local civilian population of Alconbury. Dorothy's mother volunteered for the American Red Cross, attending to the servicemen every evening at their base, with whatever they needed – cooking, washing, and nursing, too, on occasion. Many of them were very grateful, too, for the care shown by ladies like Dorothy's mother – two of them returned the kindness by helping her father complete the building of their bungalow. So much of the Second World War was a team effort in so many unexpected ways.

Dorothy Drew, November 2021.

One of the fondest memories of the war for Dorothy has to be one of the sweetest too. It relates again to the Americans, whose generosity is legendary. 'War children' like Dorothy were – for the most part – deprived of plentiful supplies of a simple joy that children today (arguably too much) take for granted: sweets.

'We just said "Gum Chum" to the Americans,' Dorothy told me, 'and out of their pockets would come Necco sweets, Herschey bars – and even bananas and oranges. When our parents said "no" they would say "yes". It is one of my favourite memories of the war.'

NOTES

1 www.factfile.org/10-facts-about-anderson-shelter
2 www.bbc.co.uk/ahistoryoftheworld/objects
3 www.wartimememoriesproject.com/ww2/airfields/airfield
4 www.iwm.org.uk/history/american-airmen-in-britain-during-the-second-world-war

ENA BOTTING:
AN AIR TRANSPORT
AUXILIARY ENGINEER

'Whoever flicked the switch that released the petrol didn't think to check there might be a young girl fiddling around under the cockpit,' Ena Botting said, rolling her eyes in incredulity, but smiling too (a little bit!) as she recalled one of the messiest memories of her days as a fitter in the Air Transport Auxiliary (ATA).[1]

This particular mishap occurred whilst Ena (née Camden), just 17 years old at the time, was checking and cleaning the petrol filters in a 'Bristol Pegasus'[2] radial engine of a twin-engine Wellington bomber, which was the main British bomber in the early part of the war, until it was supplanted later on by the larger four-engine Avro Lancaster:[3]

It was normal after an aircraft had returned to the hangar to drain out the petrol, but on this occasion some idiot came along to get the fuel, not knowing I was underneath it. I think because the filters were open the petrol came whooshing out, all over me – it stung everywhere. Luckily, I didn't have my mouth open, I usually did, I was known for being a bit of a chatterbox! The next thing I can remember is one of the male engineers scooping me up and carrying me into the ladies' bathroom and flooding cold water over me.

I was really sore for at least a few days after that, all over, and sometimes my hands and feet would swell up. I had horrid blisters on my face too. But gradually I think I stopped stinking of an old petrol can and the soreness got better.

Ena Botting was one of the ATA's 2,500 ground staff, many of whom were young women like herself wanting to 'do their bit' in the war effort. The ATA was a civilian organisation created at the beginning of the war principally to support the Royal Air Force and the Fleet Air Arm (the flying fleet of the Royal Navy, FAA) on the front line. Headquartered at White Waltham airfield in Berkshire, it was also tasked with vital maintenance and repair duties of the aircraft in its hangars. However, ATA staff also performed many other functions, including carrying service personnel from place to place (usually when the RAF were unable to do it), and air ambulance work.

It had a total staff of around 4,000 volunteers – including 1,500 pilots, ground staff, radio operators, and young Air Training Corps Cadets. Its Latin motto 'Aetheris Avidi' is literally translated as 'Eager for the Air', but its unofficial motto, 'Anything to Anywhere', is probably far more accurate. The ATA was the backbone of the RAF; without it the RAF Commands – Bomber, Fighter and Coastal – would not have been able to function. Its staff had to be extremely flexible in their approach to their work; it existed

to support, not lead, therefore all its members without exception needed to be willing to undertake whatever task was directed at them – not only 'anything to anywhere' but 'anything to anyone'.

Almost all the aircraft flown by RAF and FAA crews during the war (of which there were 147 different types, including the best-known:[3] Spitfires, Lancasters, Mustangs, Wellingtons, Halifaxes, Fairey Battles, Hurricanes, Blenheims, and Mosquitos, to name but a few) were almost certainly flown at some point by ATA staff. The ATA maintained its own fleet of taxi and training aircraft, and its ground staff ensured that all

Ena Botting, aged 17.

aircraft on delivery were pre-flight checked if in transit via an ATA ferry pool. The ATA had an amazing but little-known service record. In total, its pilots alone flew for over 415,000 hours – over 309,000 flights. Sadly 173 of them – women as well as men – lost their lives.

Given the importance of their work – and it was extremely important because the safety of RAF crews on operations were dependent on their aircraft being properly and thoroughly maintained, and of course repaired when necessary – the ATA staff received very little training specific to the type of aircraft they were maintaining or flying before they were trusted to simply 'get on with the job'. The very basic training given applied to all its staff, top to bottom – pilots down to ground staff; and – very interestingly – there was little differentiation in the training of men and women in all the jobs too.

Ena recalled how delighted she was when she was recruited into the ATA the day after her interview. She said:

It was all a bit chaotic! I was working in a dress shop in Maidenhead when I learnt that the ATA was looking for volunteers to sign up and join its team. My father told me about the opportunity – he was already working at the airfield, doing all sorts of jobs but mostly as a fireman; we had been evacuated to Maidenhead from Eltham in south-east London earlier in the war. I really wanted to do it from the moment he suggested I try. I wouldn't have minded what I did but I definitely wanted to feel more useful than I felt I was selling dresses. I had always been interested in aeroplanes too – as a little girl I used to stay with an aunt who lived not far from an airfield and although there weren't very many planes flying from it, I used to love going with her to see small aircraft take off and come back. One of my earliest childhood memories is of me doing a 'bit of a runner' from my aunt's house to see the planes by myself and I got lost on the way home. I was really told off! Now, as an 'old lady' I still love the sound of an aircraft in the sky. The moan, hum and roar of an engine sort of makes my heart sing, it makes me feel young again!

So a young girl, like me, couldn't have been more pleased when I received the message I was to be welcomed into the ATA. It was a bit of a muddle though, from the beginning – I was told to begin my work the very next day after they offered me the position – but then told that actually my first day would be a day off – and I could have the next day off as well. Anyway, I finally started three days later.

I was told then, too, that I would start my training, to be a fitter, with lessons in a sort of classroom, next to the main hangar. But when I arrived instead of having lessons a bucket full of soap and water was thrust at me, and at some of the other new girls, as well as some old rags and sponges and we were told to clean some of the planes in the hangar. They said the 'courses weren't ready to start' – that was how my ATA days began. Looking back, it was a great way to learn about the aeroplanes. And it was fun!

After a few days of scrubbing, polishing, dusting and scraping muck off fuselages and cockpits alike, Ena was told her 'teacher' was ready to begin (slightly more) formal training, in the classroom. The teaching, which went on for some weeks, led to her receiving an 'Approved Engineer's Card', graded 'semi-skilled'. It was a very practical course, during which she – and around six other young girls, including one called 'Ann' who became her 'best ATA friend', were in and out of the hangar too with the male engineers – mostly older men who had not gone on active service for health reasons, or some of whom had been especially brought into the ATA because some fully qualified engineers were needed to teach others, like Ena, who knew very little.

We (the girls) tended to work with the same engineer; mostly older men, some of them didn't think much of us, mostly because they didn't think girls of our age, with hardly any training at all, would be able to get much done – and we'd all be slow learners. But I was quite lucky, I was with a really nice man. He didn't say very much at all, I think he was very shy, but he taught me well and he really encouraged me. But some of the girls weren't so lucky, it wasn't easy when the men said things like 'it isn't right for young women to do this,' that sort of thing. But eventually they got used to us, and they had to help us get on because there weren't enough of them to look after all the planes themselves!

Ena also recalled, quite happily, how much she liked a book she was given whilst doing her studies, which helped her learn. Because she was so interested in the aircraft and its parts the book was describing, she said she 'enjoyed looking at her lovely book, with all its different tips and lots of advice'.

The little book, Ena told me, was certainly very useful – but most of the time they simply learned 'on the job'. No two days were the same and they didn't know what they would be tasked with from one day to the next.

'I didn't really mind what job I was given,' Ena told me, and continued to recall some of her most memorable moments, some of which had nothing to do with aircraft at all!

From the way Ena went on to talk about her time in the ATA in the days, weeks, and months that followed it is quite clear that no textbooks, lessons, tests or teachers could have fully prepared her for the unpredictability of her time in this vital unit, which was both chaotic and meticulously organised at the same time. She described a rich tapestry of activity; happenings centring around the aircraft that were so crucial to the war effort, that needed constant attention and which Ena, a young girl in a man's world, was thrilled to be around, whatever duty she was tasked to complete.

It was touching to hear her speak so fondly of the aircraft. 'I loved them all,' she said:

> But I couldn't help having my favourites! And my two favourite planes were the Anson and Wellington – they had so much character. I didn't like the Hurricane much, I don't know why. It deserves a lot more credit because it brought down a lot of enemy aircraft – more than the Spitfire. But everyone loved the Spitfire – they still do – because it was so beautiful. And I remember the women ATA pilots liked flying the Spitfires best; some people say the Spitfire was designed for women pilots.

Upon speaking about the Avro Anson, a twin-engine multi-use aircraft used during the war by both the RAF and the FAA, Ena remembered one of hardest jobs she was asked to do sometimes – which was to, physically, wind up the undercarriage of the Anson. In referring to the 'undercarriage' Ena was talking of the landing gear. Raising and lowering the wheels of an early Anson required about 160 turns of a handle in the cockpit. I think Ena was referring to having to check that operation in the hangar with the aircraft supported on jacks; however, when taken flying, she may also have been asked to wind it up after take-off and lower it again for landing. This was just one of many jobs she found difficult. Another was changing the wheels on an aircraft.

'I remember Ann and I trying to change the wheels on a Wellington,' she said (laughing), 'how we struggled. It was really hard!' (I have to admit, rather shamefully, I am not surprised to hear that two girls, only in their mid-teens found it tricky to change the wheels of a Vickers Wellington.[4] After all, whilst not the largest aircraft in the RAF fleet by a long shot – that accolade goes to the Lancaster – it was one of the largest: it had a wingspan of 26m and weighed (when empty) around 8,400kg.

Ena went on to explain that the ground staff, including herself, worked as either 'fitters', or 'riggers'. Fitters, generally, worked on engines and riggers on the airframe (i.e. the fuselage, undercarriage, wings etc; anything except the engine). She said she liked, most of all, working as a fitter, because aircraft engines were constantly fascinating to her, but after the petrol episode she was mostly taken off 'fitter' duties and did a lot more 'rigging', such as the jobs described above. However, neither job – of course – was more important than the other. Both fitters and riggers were part of an even bigger team, all doing their utmost to ensure all ATA's aircraft were as safe and as robust as possible. In the chain of perceived seniority, the pilot of the crew was seen as the 'top man', and the riggers and fitters were known as 'erks' at the bottom. The term 'erk' first started out as 'airk', short for aircraftman – other erks were armourers, who serviced guns and fitted bombs, and electricians, who worked on the electrical and radio systems of an aircraft.

However, that said, only a (metaphorically) short-sighted pilot would not be appreciative of the team behind him who serviced his aircraft, because his safety in the sky was entirely dependent upon their diligence. All the erks – indeed the flying crews too – needed to understand their aircraft, and very often their technical knowledge was superior to that of a pilot, navigator or even flight engineer. The knowledge gained as an erk, and the everyday practice of working on aircraft, actually resulted in some of them progressing 'up the ladder'; during the Battle of Britain almost a third of Britain's fighter pilots were originally erks.

So often, too, when we think about the dangers faced by those working with wartime aircraft, in the RAF as well as the ATA, we just think about bombing raids, when aircraft are about 20,000ft high, circling, diving and twisting, and being shot at from all angles, including by ack-ack from the ground. But there were many other hazards – even for ground crew of the ATA, including in the comparative safety of Ena's hangar. It wasn't unknown for crew to walk into spinning propellers as engines were run up (that would have been on the airfield), and all aircraft contained lethal cocktails of fuel, pressurised oxygen, ammunition, and gallons of oil.

Ena recalled a moment when a young girl, newly recruited into the ATA, lit a cigarette whilst in the hangar, standing underneath the wings of a Fairchild (UC-21 American light transport aircraft). Ena said: 'luckily most of the petrol had been drained out, but it still went up in a puff of smoke. Silly girl, she didn't do that again!'

That memory was one of the most vivid of Ena's recollections – there were others, too – which put images in my mind. One of these was about the airfield at White Waltham; for a change, not about an individual aircraft. She said:

I remember, it was a really hot day and suddenly we were all – everyone who was around regardless of their job – told to go onto the airstrip, get down on our hands and knees and pick up bits of broken glass. We all crawled around under the baking hot sun. I think some fool had put dust and rubble, which contained the glass, on the grass instead of fertiliser, and the glass had to be removed because of the wheels of the aircraft that would be landing there. It was really hard work and we didn't pick much up, and then someone else came along with a glass magnet and finished the job anyway. Very annoying!

Ena also recalled her excitement when, after cleaning an (American) Beechcraft aircraft, she was told she had prepared it for ATA Commodore Gerard d'Erlanger, who, whilst running British Airways in 1938, had come up with the idea of establishing the ATA after he foresaw a need for it because of the impact the outbreak of the war would have on civilian aircraft (with the government basically requisitioning all the planes). As well as flying himself, d'Erlanger was commodore of the ATA throughout the war. However, it was not only for Sir Gerard that Ena cleaned the Beechcraft's windows, swept its floor and emptied its ashtrays, but also for Prince Bernhard of the Netherlands, with whom d'Erlanger travelled.

She spoke fondly, too, of the friends she made – particularly Ann, who, after the war was her bridesmaid. This is one of her most delightful memories:

Ann had a lovely singing voice, and so did one of the other girls who was our friend too, but I can't remember her name now. Sometimes the two of them would sit on the wing of an aircraft and sing, and I, and the other girls, would listen. It was really lovely.

Ena said she could remember the hangar she worked in very well, too. She said:

> I can remember it so vividly I could almost draw a picture of it. It was huge. To get in we'd go through a little door and near that door was the ladies' cloak-room, then there was a large cupboard where the plug-cleaners were kept, then an instrument cupboard, then a room where all the fabrics and cleaning stuffs were kept. In the middle of the hangar were the stores, and an area for the men to hang their clothes. Then there was a door into a smaller hangar, where we ate in the canteen and next to that was the classroom. It became quite a squash when there were a lot of aircraft in there too – we had the most fun when an American plane would arrive, a B-17 Flying Fortress or something. We didn't help look after them because the Americans had their own people, but us girls had fun because they would always say to us, 'Hey, you want chocolate? Stockings?!'

Then, perhaps the memories that were the epitome of all her ATA days, Ena's flying moments. She said she couldn't remember exactly, but thinks she flew at least three times, always in a (beloved) Avro Anson. She had little warning when she was going to be taken up – just that her boss would occasionally say suddenly, 'Yours is going up, get in!' She said she was terribly sick the first time she flew, but then it got better for her. She recalled one particular flight over Windsor, near the castle (but not over it because that was not allowed), which was where she took the controls … what a moment, indeed, for 17-year-old Ena Botting.

However, in writing of female pilots – which Ena was, for a fleeting moment – this chapter, indeed a book about remarkable women of the Second World War, would be incomplete without a mention of the (civilian) female pilots who flew for the ATA.[5] The ATA's female aircrew totalled 164 pilots – known as 'Atagirls' – and four flight engineers. They were expected to – and did – undertake the same tasks as the male pilots, which included ferrying aircraft from factories to the front line, usually completely alone. They had to be pre-pared, and able, to fly whichever aircraft needed to be transported, and this included the RAF's 'biggest and mightiest', such beasts of the sky as the four-engine Lancaster bomber, as well as the smaller Spitfires. It was completely unprecedented, then, for women to fly such aircraft, but they did so because they had to, and they demonstrated the same levels of skill and courage as the men – proven by the successful deliveries they made.

However, unsurprisingly perhaps, the concept of a young woman flying an enormous aircraft entirely alone was often not easily accepted by their male counterparts, either in the RAF or the ATA. There is a well-documented episode where there was a 'hunt' for the pilot of a just-delivered Wellington bomber, because the aircrew it had been taken to simply did not believe it could have been flown by a woman. But it was; it was flown by Mary Ellis, just 5ft 2in tall, who had delivered it for it to fly on a front-line operation. In her memoir, *A Spitfire Girl*, Mary Ellis wrote that they 'didn't believe I was the pilot of the Wellington. One or two of them still decided to clamber on up the ladder to check the aeroplane for the "missing" pilot … They just could not believe women could fly these planes.'[6]

In all, Mary Ellis, who achieved the ATA rank of First Officer by the end of the war, flew over 1,000 times, in seventy-six different types of plane (including a Spitfire over 400 times), from around 200 different airfields from 1942 to the war's end in 1945.

Indeed, it is extraordinary to think of a petite young woman being able to fly such an aircraft – often of course in terrible weather and/or in reach of the enemy. However, Ena's descriptions of such things as fixing the oil system of a Fairchild (which she did, she said, by first of all checking the oil cylinder) remind us that young women could be highly proficient engineers too, when the need arose. She also told me: 'The lid of the oil cylinder (a plug) had two holes in it into which the spanner fitted, so that the plug could be unscrewed and removed. I had that spanner for many years, but sadly can't find it now.'

Writing of admiration brings me neatly, almost, to the end of Ena's ATA story, and the end of her Second World War, because this is when she met Jesse Botting, to whom she was married for sixty-seven years. They married in May 1945; he died in 2012. Jesse was seconded to the ATA from the RAF shortly before the end of the war, after serving in 23 Squadron in Fighter Command. He was then posted to an air-sea rescue squadron, before joining the ATA at the end of the war as a radio operator – the ATA were not allowed to fly outside of the UK without an RAF Wireless Operator. This was significant towards the end of the war because the ATA were ferrying lots of people to and from the Continent, including many French, Dutch, and Belgian citizens who wanted to return to their home countries, after fleeing to Britain whilst their countries were occupied from the summer of 1940 to 1944.

Jesse and Ena Botting were but two members of the ATA, the Command that nobly served behind the scenes of the Royal Air Force, performing a crucial function, every single day. We have as much to thank Jesse and Ena for as we do Sir Gerard d'Erlanger and Mary Ellis. At the end of the war, Lord Beaverbrook, the wartime Minister of Aircraft Production, gave the ATA a fitting tribute, declaring:

> Without the ATA the days and nights of the Battle of Britain would have been conducted under conditions quite different from the actual events. They carried out the delivery of aircraft from the factories to the RAF, thus relieving countless numbers of RAF pilots for duty in the battle. Just as the Battle of Britain is the accomplishment and achievement of the RAF, likewise it can be declared that the ATA sustained and supported them in the battle. They were soldiers fighting in the struggle just as completely as if they had been engaged on the battlefront.[7]

NOTES

1 atamuseum.org
2 www.wondersofworldaviation.com/bristol_pegasus
3 Bill Gunston, *Aircraft of World War 2*, Octopus Books Ltd, 1980
4 www.baesystems.com/en/heritage/vickers-wellington
5 Mary Ellis and Melody Foreman, *A Spitfire Girl: The World's Greatest Female Ferry Pilot Tells Her Story*, Frontline books, 2016
6 Ibid
7 atamuseum.org/ve-day-and-ata

VERA SAIES: A BATTLE OF BRITAIN PLOTTER

Just before 7 a.m. on 15 September 1940, 27-year-old Vera Saies descended the seventy-six steps that took her down to the concrete bunker that was the Royal Air Force Operations Room in Uxbridge, West London.[1] The Battle of Britain was reaching its height, but Vera had no idea as she entered the Bunker that morning what a hugely important day it was to become.

Vera worked in the Bunker as a 'plotter', one of 120 Women's Auxiliary Air Force (WAAF) members, employed under the leadership of 11 Group of Fighter Command,[2] to help guide RAF aircraft to victory during this most crucial battle of the skies.

The significance of the concentrated work undertaken in this Room – which, hidden 60ft underground and with 1m-thick walls, was clammy and claustrophobic at the best of times – should never be underestimated. It was the beating heart of Fighter Command; it was from here that the Battle of Britain was effectively fought and won. As well as the large table covered in a map of the area of battle upon which Vera, and her colleagues, would use wooden croupier-style pushing sticks to mark where aircraft were after receiving information that came through to them on telephones and through their headsets, there was a display board. The board was constantly being updated, showing where all Allied squadrons and – crucially – enemy squadrons were at any given time. With so much information being visible, precise instructions could be issued from this Bunker to squadron leaders about where and when they should fly and attack.

Thankfully the 'beating heart' of Fighter Command successfully pumped blood into the vital organs that were the aircraft of the Spitfire and Hurricane squadrons it commanded throughout the whole of the Battle Britain – between 10 July and 31 October 1940. However, 15 September 1940 has since been remembered as 'Battle of Britain Day'[3] because this was the day German High Command instructed its air force, the Luftwaffe, to attack London on an unprecedented scale. Up to this point, during the previous weeks of the Battle of Britain, the Luftwaffe had attacked various targets in the United Kingdom with a considerable degree of success but had not achieved the invasion that was their goal.

The Luftwaffe launched two massive attacks on London in September: the first on the 7th and the second – the larger of the two – on the 15th. It is thought that Germany assumed RAF strength and resources had been depleted to the extent they would not be able to withstand another day of intense bombing. But they were wrong. RAF Fighter Command squadrons were at their most determined and most prepared, and by the end of the day it was clear that the Luftwaffe had failed to achieve the air supremacy they needed to invade. It was the first major defeat of the Second World War for Hitler.

Vera Shaw (her married name) died in April 2001, aged 89. Thankfully – since such memories help us better understand the complexity and brilliance that led the RAF to victory during the Battle of Britain – Vera took the trouble to record some of her most poignant recollections before she died. Her daughter Laurette has kindly shared some of these extraordinary memories with me for this book. Of that especially memorable day in 1940, Laurette told me:

My mother reported for duty, as normal, in the morning of 15 September. Sshe and the other girls were reading, knitting or doing other similar things to occupy themselves whilst they waited to start work … but there was a commotion, and she dropped her book on the floor and ran over to the tele-printer. It contained a message about waves of bombers heading for the heart of London. At first, the sergeant in charge did not believe what she was reading and asked her to read the message twice. But what she was reading was true, German bombers were heading to London, in huge numbers. My mother was one of the first to find out just how many were on their way.

She told me she started work straightaway, 'plotting' with other girls, not even thinking of stopping at midday when her shift should have ended.

Mother also recalled that both King George VI and the Prime Minister Winston Churchill, with Mrs Churchill, visited the Operations Room that day. Churchill made a point of not disturbing or interrupting the vital work that was happening (at great speed), but she did recall that at one stage the Prime Minister – seeing the number of enemy planes identified on the table – asked if there were any reserve fighters to be called upon. He was told the answer was 'no' because all our aircraft were already in the air. This, obviously, worried him terribly, but my mother said he didn't overreact and they just carried on with their work.

Later that day, when it became clear that the RAF had won the day over the Luftwaffe, my mother described a wonderful moment when the Prime Minister, and his wife Clementine, congratulated all the team in the bunker. She said he was in an exceptionally good mood, smiling and waving at everyone. All the time he was puffing away on his cigar which he wasn't allowed to do, but no one minded.

In Laurette's words, gathered from notes made by her mother, there was huge relief and excitement amongst all those working in the bunker at the end of the day:

15th September proved that the pilots of the RAF were far from beaten. They remained masters of the day-time skies over Britain. Two days later Hitler postponed indefinitely his plans for an invasion. German bombers would return to London and other cities every night for months in an attempt to break the spirit of the British people, but civilians carried on in the Blitz as they had begun the Battle of Britain – determined to add to the victory of the 'Few', the 'Victory of the Many'.

Vera Shaw was one of the first of around 1,500 young women to join the WAAF[4] when it was created at the end of June in 1939. In her assessment process Laurette told me her mother was initially tested for the task of photographic identification and analysis, but because she was quite short-sighted this was ruled out, so, instead, she trained as a plotter at a WAAF training centre in West Drayton, London. The Battle of Britain was possibly the most hectic few weeks for the plotters and RAF staff at Uxbridge, but they worked meticulously throughout the whole of the war including during the evacuation of Dunkirk, throughout the Blitz and on D-Day.

'However,' Laurette said:

> My mother didn't sign up to the WAAF thinking about plotting or reconnaissance or anything like that. I am sure she wanted to do something useful, but what she really liked about the WAAF was the uniform! She was a well-dressed lady, always quite fashion-conscious – I remember her telling me that she thought the blue of the WAAF clothes was far prettier than the rather dull khaki outfit she would have had to wear if she had joined the Auxiliary Territorial Service, the 'sister' organisation of the WAAF's in the Army. Some years after the war I visited the Bunker with Mother (it is now a museum) and the gentleman showing us round said his mother had joined the WAAF too, for the same reason. Mother was much amused …
>
> It was after this visit that another – sort of charming – anecdote slipped out. Mother told me that as often as possible, whatever was going on after work she and her WAAF friends would travel into London for an evening out. The girls weren't allowed to wear civilian clothes and were also forbidden to wear make-up whilst in uniform. These rules didn't suit my mother and her friends at all and, once they reached the city, they would change into pretty frocks instead, put some make-up on and leave their uniform in left luggage lockers. In the early part of the war, one evening she drove into town in her own small car, with a friend, duly changed and after their evening had ended, drove back to Uxbridge – but through an air raid. They were delayed, arriving back at their digs later than permitted. Choosing not to face a reprimand, which they would have had they gone through the main gate and past the Guard Room, the two of them climbed a fence into their camp. They crept in, found their beds and – without putting the lights on – went to bed. In the morning they were surprised to discover they were completely alone. There was an unexploded bomb in the camp, and everyone had been evacuated, so they were caught!

★★★

The WAAF grew quickly after it was launched, taking on around 2,000 new recruits each week, reaching a peak of over 180,000 women by the summer of 1943. The WAAFs undertook a huge variety of positions – some packed and repaired parachutes, while others worked in catering, cooking, washing up, sourcing food for servicemen. Many had positions more closely aligned with the actual aircraft and flying – such as studying the weather and providing meteorological reports, monitoring and reporting on radar, carrying out maintenance on aircraft and of aircraft parts. Communication duties included wireless and telephonic operations, others examined reconnaissance, and some were even involved in intelligence operations.

Even though WAAFs did not participate in active combat and were not employed as aircrew (apart from female pilots who transported aircraft from factories to the front-line as members of the ATA), those who worked at military installations were exposed to some of the same dangers as men; and, sadly, by the end of the war some 1,570 members of ground crew WAAF's had died in service. Some of the greatest risks they were exposed to were within Balloon Command,[5] an RAF Command established to employ men, and women, to help protect cities and key industrial targets with the harnessing of large inflatable balloons that were fixed to the ground with the purpose of deflecting enemy dive bombers, pushing the bombers higher than they would have been wanting to fly and shielding targets from incendiary bombs and other explosives.

It was only female nurses whose work for the RAF did not fall under the auspices of the WAAF; they, instead, belonged to the Princess Mary's Royal Air Force Nursing Service; which employed around 70,000 nurses around the world, in addition to some 10,000 young women who worked in reserve positions.

The WAAFs, in whatever role they had, worked long, hard hours, and were mostly paid around two thirds of what their male contemporaries were. Vera, as a 'Plotter', protected by the concrete walls and far underground whilst in the Bunker, was shielded from bombing that may have been going on above her, but nonetheless whilst on shift the work was often relentlessly stressful; even when exhausted, 'plotters' had to be alert, constantly concentrating, listening, and reacting instantaneously to the messages they received.

Describing her mother's work at RAF Uxbridge, Laurette told me:

The plotters worked in shifts called 'watches'; my mother was in Number 1 of four watches. There were thirty in each group. They wore headphones and took in information from a filter room which gave them numbers, height, and direction of approaching enemy aircraft. A chain of radar stations on the coast were the first to spot potential enemy activity but those taking in the radar reports had to be careful as a large flock of birds could give a similar outline to aircraft. Anyway, the radar reports, together with information from the Royal Observer Corps on the ground and intelligence sources was fed through to the filter room which then assessed the situation and passed this directly to the plotters.

The plotters then had to plot both enemy and friendly plane numbers and positions on the large plot table, which was divided into seven sectors, where the RAF fighter squadrons were based – at Kenley, North Weald, Debden, Biggin Hill, Tangmere, Hornchurch and Northolt. Using their long 'plotting poles', they pushed blocks, clearly distinguishing between enemy and RAF, with numbers of planes in the relevant sectors. On a huge board in front of the table were the details of all the different squadrons of fighters and their airfields; lights indicated which fighters were on the ground and which were in the sky. Overlooking the plotting table, behind the glass, were three tiers of desks. At the top was the Commander of 11 Group (during the Battle of Britain this was Air Vice-Marshall Keith Park, a New Zealander). Below the Commander, on the lower two tiers, were other RAF personnel. They could all see the map in front of them and the position of aircraft, which helped them decide which Squadrons should take to the sky, and where they should go.

As mentioned above, 15 September was an extremely significant day, hugely memorable for all those involved at Uxbridge, of course, but also for the hundreds of aircrews who took to the battle in the sky. However, 18 August 1940 is another significant date in the Battle of Britain calendar. It doesn't have the notoriety of being 'Battle of Britain Day' but it is remembered as 'The Hardest Day' because of the numbers of aircraft – enemy and Allied – that were lost: around seventy and sixty respectively. Germany, however, lost far more men: over ninety were killed on that day alone.

Accurate plotting, which led to information going up the chain of command and passed to those in the sky firing gun and dropping bombs, was – therefore – vital in the overcoming of the Luftwaffe. In Vera's words:

It was so chaotic at the time and so noisy in the Ops Room that there wasn't much time to think about the German planes in terms of the people inside them …We were delighted when our fighters intercepted them. We just wanted the war to end.

An extraordinary reunion was arranged for Vera exactly thirty-eight years after The Hardest Day – on 18 August 1978. Vera was reunited with a German airman whom her 'plotting' had caused him to bail out of his Dornier bomber into the English Channel. The Luftwaffe pilot, Günther Unger, went to the meeting, which was at RAF Uxbridge, and (as reported in the *Daily Mail* on Saturday, 19 August 1978) to that day thinking of The Hardest Day always made his skin tingle. Unger is quoted as saying:

> It was the first time I'd lost a plane but fortunately none of our crew of four was injured. We had dropped our bombs on Kenley airfield and had been hit by flak on our way home. Over the Channel we were engaged by a Hurricane. We were badly hit and had to ditch before we were picked up by a German ship.[6]

Vera Saies, c. 1941.

Vera was stationed at Uxbridge until the summer of 1941, after which she received a commission and transferred to Number 5 Group of Bomber Command based in Grantham, Lincolnshire. Here, she commanded a section of WAAF girls, ensuring they did whatever was required of them to support the male officers and crews serving in the fifteen (or so) squadrons that were in 5 Group; there was never a dull moment!

This group undertook some of the most important raids of the Second World War –including the Dambusters Raid (also known as Operation Chastise) led by 617 Squadron, which also led the group. This raid was named for the three dams in the Ruhr Valley that the new, top-secret 'bouncing bomb' destroyed, and it resulted in massive damage to electricity supplies and war production in the area.

However, away from the frontline Vera also had domestic duties to contend with – and it was whilst trying to deal with issues of damp in the house she and some of the girls were billeted in that her life took a quite unexpected turn. She asked the RAF Medical Officer Wing Commander Donald Shaw to look at some of the worst of the mould growing in the house, such was her concern about the health of those in her care. He duly did, after which he asked Vera out for dinner. Laurette told me, 'My mother accepted immediately; and the rest (to quote a cliché) is history – they were married in February 1943.'

From talking to Laurette and reading the notes she gave me, I think it would be fair to conclude that the Second World War was a rewarding, fascinating but inevitably challenging time for Vera. Laurette told me her mother loved to meet all sorts of people and of course the war brought her into contact with many. In a document Vera gave to her family, she wrote:

The WAAF came from all walks of life. On my watch with 11 Group in Uxbridge we had a writer, a hospital almoner, a medical student, a secretary, and others who had been doing social or voluntary work at home.

If we had cars, we were allowed to keep them on the camp until petrol coupons were withdrawn. Being young and foolish we often drove up to London, sometimes when the blackout made it hard to see. There was not, of course, much traffic around.

We had parades but seldom attended, having the excuse of either being on duty or resting before the next session.

Whilst at Uxbridge, we were about thirty on a 'watch', with two NCOs (newly commissioned officers) and I lived in what had been an officer's house – one watch to a house. We had to light our boiler for the hot water and the house in the winter was very cold. At the top of the 'ops room' was our rest room, a small coffee shop which we had to run ourselves because of security.

I hope this gives you a slight account of our life as 'Clerks Special Duties' as we were known.

I think we all enjoyed our most interesting work.

★★★

Laurette has suggested that if Vera was still alive and knew her story was being published, she would like it to be dedicated to her friends and colleagues in the WAAF. In the words of the WAAF Association:

In dedication to all past and serving airwomen of the RAF who served at home and abroad, we pledge our friendship; and to those who lost their lives, remembrance.

We will remember them.

NOTES

1 www.battleofbritainbunker.co.uk
2 Patrick Bishop, *Bomber Boys: Fighting Back 1940–1945*, Harper Perennial, 2008
3 Simon Pearson and Ed Gorman, *Battle of Britain*, Hodder and Stoughton, 2020
4 www.rafmuseum.org.uk/research/online-exhibitions/women-of-the-air-force/
5 www.forces.net/news/aviation-history/barrage-balloons-what-were-raf-squadrons-which-defended-wwii-britain
6 *Daily Mail*, Saturday, 19 August 1978

CLARICE JACQUES: THE STORY OF A ROYAL AIR FORCE NURSE

UNITED KINGDOM

BELGIUM

English Channel

GERMANY

Lille

Arromanches, where Clarice arrived, is about here

LUX

Rouen

Reims

Metz

Caen

Nancy

Strasbourg

Brest

Paris○

Approximate location of the 'Falaise Pocket'

Orléans

Angers

Tours

Dijon

Nantes

FRANCE

SWITZERLAND

Atlantic Ocean

Limoges

Clermont-Ferrand

Lyon

Grenoble

ITALY

Bordeaux

Nîmes

Nice

Montpellier

Toulouse

Marseille

Pau

Toulon

Perpignan

100 km

N

60 mi

SPAIN

Mediterranean Sea

○→□ Eckert IV

Base map of France via d-maps.com: d-maps.com/carte.php?num_car=18005&lang=en

At daybreak we saw the shores of Normandy, at Arromanches. The huge Mulberry harbour, much of it broken up by Channel gales, was pitching and tossing up and down with the heave of the waves. The LCT [Landing Craft Tank], upon which we were boarded, docked at a prefabricated pier, opened its great jaws and lorries drove out from its hold, one by one. The vehicles on the deck were brought down in the lift.

I was in the car with an adjutant and one other nurse. Having driven down the ramp, we had to traverse a long narrow floating causeway, which was partly under water, to reach the shore. The adjutant was a good driver, and we made it safely onto the beach, where we drove up a slight rise to firmer shell-holed ground above.

August 23rd, 1944. We were in Normandy at last.

Now that General Montgomery's divisions had broken through the German defences at Caen, and the Americans had swept round to close the Falaise Gap, the Battle of Normandy was virtually over. The RAF was at last able to have more airfields in France, and our Mobile Field Hospitals were there to look after them.

The above words have been given to me for this book by Rosie Ives, whose mother, Clarice, was a nurse throughout the whole of the Second World War. Rosie helped her mother write up her wartime memories before she died in 2009, aged 97. Together they produced a beautifully written memoir for family and friends called *Travels with a Gasmask*.[1]

Rosie sent me her mother's story after I contacted the Women's Auxiliary Air Force Association, appealing for a nursing memory to help me illustrate the chapter I so want, and need, to include in *Remarkable Women of the Second World War*. Without such a chapter this book would, I feel, be incomplete. I was so pleased, therefore, to receive a copy of *Travels with a Gasmask* from Rosie. Clarice's words relate the experience of thousands, millions, of women who – day after day – during the Second World War bathed wounds, administered medicine, mopped fevered brows, squeezed the hands of the dying and patiently sat with those tormented with pain. Nurses of the Second World War, no matter where they were or whichever service they were in, saved millions of lives; but they also will have managed, many times, to enable a more peaceful death to those whose lives could not be saved.

I am so pleased that Rosie sent me this book, written for their family, but which she has now decided would like to be more widely shared. We can only know the reality of experience through the truth and this what Clarice has given us. Rosie writes in a note at the end of her mother's story, 'My mother knew her story was an important part of nursing history and women in war.' I couldn't agree more. Through Clarice's words we can stop and think, realistically, about what it might have been like to be a young nurse, working in a busy hospital when suddenly life is thrown into disarray and fear is around every corner …

So, before I go any further, thank you Rosie for giving me your mother's story; and thank you Clarice for all you did. This is an account of one 'remarkable' nurse; and it is important – as Rosie reminds us – because her words shine a light on the experience of so many.

★★★

I chose to open Clarice's chapter with her arrival in France in the summer of 1944 because, from reading her story, there is no doubt that this was a hugely significant moment for her – not only perhaps the most poignant moment of the war for young Clarice, but a memory that remained with her for the rest of her life.

And we should not be surprised by this. At the time, August 1944, Clarice Jacques was 33 years old. She was a nurse of considerable experience and ability but never before had her skills been put to the test on foreign shores. Emotionally, and practically, she was somewhat prepared for the new challenges that lay ahead; her home town of Ipswich and the surrounding areas had not escaped the war; being bombed too, each attack bringing injured, tortured troops and civilians to the East Suffolk and Ipswich hospital where she worked for the first two years of the war, a steep learning curve that not only increased her workload but also strengthened her resolve to do all she could to relieve the pain and suffering of those who needed her.

Clarice writes in *Travels with a Gasmask* of what she and her nursing friends were asked to do after war was announced, on 3 September 1939, to prepare for the worst. She describes how they rushed around putting blackout blinds in windows, set up Air Raid Precaution (ARP) groups, organised the distribution of gas masks and ration cards; and attended training sessions about what to do – and how to look after patients – in the event of an air-raid siren (or 'banshee') sounding. Whilst these preparations were essential, they disrupted their everyday work, and all the nurses could do was try to cope in the best way. She wrote, for example, that quite often the sirens would ring in the morning. Recalling the first time it happened during a morning clinic, she wrote:

We ushered the walking patients in as orderly a manner as possible over the short distance to our designated space. It was only partly below ground as the wards above were built on a slope. We were crowded in shoulder to shoulder, and with fear and trembling, waited for the first bombs to fall. For half an hour nothing happened. Then we heard the blast of the 'all clear' siren and returned to the department to continue where we had left off.

With all the morning's work disrupted, it became rather a shambles – nurses had stayed with stretcher cases and consultants had refused to shelter anyway. We were late preparing for the afternoon clinics, which caused further confusion.

General chaos and fear continued to penetrate the nurses' days during these early weeks of war, but it wasn't long before its true and painful reality struck. In the middle of November 1939, a ship carrying Dutch and Belgian refugees fleeing their countries in the face of the advancing Germans was struck by a mine whilst crossing the North Sea. Men, women and children were thrown into the water and many – those fortunate enough to be rescued – were brought to Clarice and the nurses at the East Suffolk and Ipswich Hospital. She wrote:

Notice of their impending arrival was short, but we assembled every available spare bed and stretcher. The wards were already full, so the long corridors were used as a temporary measure. It was then we felt the war had begun in earnest.

Often, sadly, nurses (doctors and surgeons too) cannot save those for whom they are caring. Not being a medic, I don't, personally, know how it feels to care for someone and then lose them, but learning how to manage this, more so than ever during the war because of the casualty rate, was another learning curve nurses had to make. I was struck by what Clarice wrote during the uncertain weeks of the Battle of Britain:

I remember one badly injured pilot among others being brought in. Because of his multiple injuries, he was taken straight to the consultant surgeon for examination and treatment. He was still conscious as the porter wheeled him to the Accident Ward. There was nothing anyone could say to him – he knew and we knew he would be lucky to survive. As I walked by the side of his trolley, I held his hand and he grasped it gratefully. Sympathetic words would have been out of place.

Clarice did not reveal in her book if this patient lived or died, but I don't think we really need to know. To me, what is so significant about this reflection is the comfort she was able to give this injured man during his time of suffering, with the simple act of taking his hand. Because of that action he was either comforted in death or strengthened to live. Such acts of tenderness, undoubtedly expressed by thousands of nurses throughout the whole of the Second World War, would – I think we can be confident of – have given immeasurable comfort to thousands in the wake of unimaginable suffering.

★★★

In the autumn of 1942 Clarice, together with some of the other sisters at her hospital, decided to apply to join a military nursing service. Not only was she (as she writes in her book) becoming 'restless' because of having worked in the same hospital for so many years, she was – of course – aware of much of what was happening in Europe, and she felt she wanted, and needed, to do more.

Clarice applied to join the Princess Mary Royal Air Force Nursing Service (PMRAFNS)[2] and was quickly accepted. There began a couple of years of working and training in several locations in England, including at RAF Innsworth in Gloucestershire, where she and her colleagues stayed in Nissen huts; here she recalled getting such a terrible sore throat her tonsils were removed – which proved for her to be the 'most painful operation one could imagine'.

Sometime after her recovery from her throat operation Clarice was posted to Blackpool, which, together with Lytham St Anne's, was the centre for the RAF Training Command. She was here for almost a year and half, during which she and the other nurses were kept busy treating the wounded and sick

Clarice Jacques, *c.* 1940.
(Sister Clarice E. Carter).

at the on-site medical centre, whilst also recalling some memorably happy times. Clarice wrote about the fish and chip stalls and amusement arcades on the South Shore, a Wurlitzer organ that blasted out tunes while they danced in the Tower Ballroom, the long stretches of 'wonderful' sandy beaches and the concert hall at the Winter Gardens. She also wrote about the men they cared for from the Polish unit, most interestingly what they learnt from them:

> In order to communicate with the Poles, we made up our own phonetic-phrase books with the help of those who spoke a little English. I remember that 'dobranoc' was 'goodnight'. We also had phonetic phrases for 'have you any pain?' and 'are you feeling better?' They were a cheerful crowd, and we had many laughs.

It was during this time, though, that she suffered with some quite serious health problems herself, including reacting badly to a TB jab that resulted in dangerously high fever, getting bitten on her face by a bedbug whilst asleep in her digs in Blackpool, which caused such infection she had a week off, and appendicitis. Her own pain and illness serve as a useful reminder, I think, that often the nurses themselves needed caring for too.

However, it was whilst she was in the mess at Blackpool, in the spring of 1944, that she saw a list of stations to which the nurses could apply for an overseas posting. By this time several of her friends had been transferred abroad, mostly to the Middle East, Africa, and Italy. Clarice wrote that she was 'beginning to feel somewhat bored and far removed from the war activity'. After carefully considering how and where she might be most useful, principally because of her operating theatre experience, she applied to join a Mobile Field Hospital (MFH) unit. She was duly accepted, after which she began her training with other Princess Mary nurses in Sussex, eventually arriving in France in August 1944.

★★★

The Second World War was at this time entering its final stages (although of course that was not then known) and France was very slowly trying to recover from the strange-hold of four years of German occupation. D-Day[3] had taken place just over ten weeks before Clarice's arrival, beginning the liberation of most – but not all – of the country, but leaving behind the chaotic aftermath of battle; hundreds of injured troops needing care and many displaced French country folk, lost, confused – and longing for somewhere to call home.

This is what greeted Clarice, now 33 years old, on her arrival in France. There was no escape for her from the war – the consequences of what had happened to this country during its occupation and during its liberation were laid bare, all around – and at the same time I am sure she would have been acutely aware that danger was still ever-present. The Second World War was not over.

But there was no escape, either, because actually – even if she had wanted to – she had nowhere to escape to. Joining an MFH unit meant that as well as literally creating the wards and temporary 'operating theatres', they also had to make their own accommodation. Everything had to be established from scratch, wherever they were needed. She wrote that on the first night they built their campsite on the common of a small village near Caen, called Cambes-en-Plaine. The Germans, she wrote:

We were about eight miles away, fleeing to the north. As soon as we arrived, we helped to pitch the main wards and theatre marquees etc, it was 'all hands

52

on deck' whenever we set up camp. The poles and canvas were laid out, and everyone had a rope to pull on when the word was given. As the big marquee rose from the ground, one had to hold onto the rope like 'grim death' until the tent pegs were fixed. Then the mess tents went up and finally the sleeping tents. Having helped unload the hospital equipment, we had to then erect our own ridge tents – two camp beds to each tent. The other officer's tents were put up by two batmen – we grumbled a little at this because we were so tired. And the weather was hot – flies and mosquitos bit viciously – and soon we were coping with outbreaks of diarrhoea among men from the airfields, and some of our staff. The slaughter in the Falaise Gap had left thousands of dead bodies of men and animals, creating a fertile breeding ground for the flies.

Clarice and the members of her unit spent the next ten days or so at this camp; she leaves to our imagination the nature of the intense nursing she provided – but we can be left in no doubt at all that it would have been as traumatic as it was exhausting. She mentions the long hours she and her nursing colleagues worked, saying they had no regular 'off-duty' time, but managed to take a few hours perhaps once a week. She wrote about:

> The local people, whose lives had been so completely disrupted and who were looking for a purpose. One villager was wandering around on the common. He had a basket on his hip and was strewing something, probably cattle-food. With his broad-brimmed straw hat, he looked for all the world just like a picture of a labourer from the Middle Ages.

She also wrote about the kindliness of the local women, who gave them carnations to decorate the 'wards'; and, of the way these same women tended three temporary graves, with wooden crosses, bearing the names and identity numbers of the British servicemen who were buried there. Each one would be later interred at an official cemetery.

Clarice also mentioned that she, and a couple of nursing friends, managed during this time to get to Bayeux (which was relatively undamaged); their hope was to see the famous 'Bayeux Tapestry' – which they found (not surprisingly) had been carefully put away for the duration of the war, but they were not too disappointed because a copy could be seen, painted on linen and draped around chairs in the cathedral.

However, their brief visit to Bayeux and the touching gestures bestowed on them by les Françaises could not protect them from the horror of war; and at this time and in this location, particularly, it was the legacy of the slaughter in the Falaise Gap that, despite the heat, chilled them to the bone.

This battle started on 8 August and continued for just under two weeks, during which time some 10,000 German troops lost their lives and a further 50,000 were captured, after being trapped in this small area – only around 50 square miles in total – which lay south of the city of Caen. The trapped Germans were relentlessly bombarded by artillery, bombed and strafed from the air. It was the final area of France the Allies needed to take for them to be able to take Paris – after which the Germans had no option but to surrender.

It was, from all accounts, a complete bloodbath; I can only think it must have been a very sobering experience indeed for Clarice, and her nursing friends, to be so physically close to the scene of such destruction. She wrote:

> The Falaise Gap had been almost sealed on 20th August, trapping most of the German Army left in Normandy. Our Commanding Officer went to the area and when he came back, he described the chaos. He said there were mangled bodies and tanks everywhere. We were told it was not fit for us to see … in every age war has been savage and horrible; only now the concentration of the slain was greater than ever.

General Dwight Eisenhower, who served as the Allied Supreme Commander of the Allied Expeditionary Force in Europe, later said of Falaise:[4]

> This was unquestionably one of the greatest 'killing fields' of any of the war areas. Forty-eight hours after the closing of the gap I was conducted through it on foot, to encounter scenes that could be described only by Dante. It was literally possible to walk for hundreds of yards at a time, stepping on nothing but dead and decaying flesh.

Eventually, after a long and exhausting packing up process, they set off for their next destination – Londinières – some 130 miles away to the east, en route to Belgium. Clarice wrote that during this journey they travelled through the city of Caen, which was not retaken by the Allies until 19 July 1944 and only after a horrific six-week battle during which around 6,000 tons of bombs were dropped on the city, killing many civilians and destroying much of the infrastructure. Clarice wrote: 'The damage was indescribable. A rough way had been cleared on the main route through the city, with rubble piled high on either side. The smell of death was everywhere; despite the heat, we just had to keep our windows closed.'

She recalled, too, the local people who watched their convoy go by, and how 'sad and sullen they appeared. Having their country invaded firstly by the Germans and then by the Allies must have been very disheartening; one could understand their feelings as they experienced so much disruption and upheaval.'

Londinières was equally challenging, albeit in different ways. Clarice wrote of how they had to set up camp in the rain, and how they worked extremely long hours treating casualties many of whom she thinks had been caught up in preparations for the Battle of Arnhem. These men 'kept the operating theatre going all night until about 5 am, as lots of them needed immediate treatment'. It was here, too, that Clarice wrote of how hungry they became because supplies – also of fresh water – were held up, and how they just had biscuits to eat, and 'awful' chlorinated water. However, in contrast to the water she so hated she mentions the cocoa they were given – infused with a dash of rum – on their departure from Londonières, again in pouring rain.

★★★

Clarice Jacques's journey serving in the Princess Mary Royal Air Force Nursing Service continued for about another ten weeks, in villages in Belgium and Brussels, during which, because it was winter, they were billeted in houses or flats. It was whilst she was in Brussels, in December 1944, that she was left in a state of shock as a V2 rocket fell onto a block of flats next to the hospital whilst she was dressing a wound. Describing her shock, but also how she and the other nurses simply had to keep going, she wrote:

> Suddenly, there was a great flash of light, followed a few seconds later by an enormous explosion which shattered the windows of the long ward and shook the ground violently. Instinctively, when the flash of light came, my patient pulled me down on to the bed and bent himself over me – a reaction which protected both of us from flying glass. We were unhurt, as were the rest of the patients, but there was broken glass everywhere as the windows caved in.

Everyone wondered where the bomb had fallen. After helping to strip the beds and clean up all the broken glass in the ward, we continued our work as usual until we went off duty. Then we saw what had happened, and what a narrow escape we had had.

Near the hospital a block of flats had been demolished – right next to the one we nurses occupied. Those off duty had not been hurt but all the windows of our flats had been blown out, including the glass-panelled doors leading to our rooms. Our beds were covered in glass splinters. The weather was cold and a continual blast of cold wind blew through the holes in the building. Although we put extra blankets on our beds, we had little sleep that night.

Our thankfulness for the safety of ourselves and our patients and colleagues was overshadowed by the death and destruction next door to us as we looked down into the deep hole left by the bomb.

Clarice's overseas posting ended at the beginning of January 1945; shortly after this she became ill with gastritis and sick leave forced her to retire from service before the end of the war. That is how her *Travels with a Gasmask* came to an end.

She was one of just under 500 nurses who served in the PMRAFNS through-out the war, not only in European countries including France and Italy, but further afield in Africa, the Middle East and India. PMRAFNS nurses still actively support the Royal Air Force; the service is now over 100 years old – having been established in 1918. The Army and the Royal Navy both, too, have their own nursing services, in the Queen Alexandra's Royal Army Nursing Corps, and the Queen Alexandra's Royal Naval Nursing Service.

All of these nursing services provided immensely valuable support day after day during the war, wherever they were, in whatever health the nurses them-selves were, and with whatever they had. The military nurses were but a small percentage of the enormous army of women across the world who served lovingly, diligently, exhaustively, in equal measure. At the beginning of the war in Great Britain alone a Civil Nursing Reserve was set up which trained around 7,000 young women to be nurses and a further 3,000 as assistant nurses. In addition, about another 60,000 women signed up to be on-hand to help air-raid casualties.

However, their status – civilian or military – did not matter; what matters is what they did. What matters is the care they provided, the comfort they bestowed and the healing they delivered.

***

Clarice Jacques's Second World War story is also important because of something else that happened to her. Something that happened to thousands and thousands of women during the war, regardless of where they were, what they were doing or which 'side' they were on.

Clarice became pregnant by a highly decorated Spitfire pilot, a Wing Commander from New Zealand, who offered her a drink and a dance at a party for RAF servicemen at the local airfield in Courtrai, in Belgium. Apparently, Rosie told me, the Germans had departed at great haste, leaving behind copious amounts of wine and champagne.

Clarice writes very little about her child's father, saying only, 'I immediately felt at ease with him.' It was not until reading her daughter Rosie's notes at the end of the book did I realise Clarice fell pregnant that night, because Rosie was born at the end of June 1945. Rosie wrote:

> My mother looked after me for a year before she placed me in a lovely Children's Home in Hampstead, so she could get back to work nearby and then go to Suffolk, to be with her mother.
>
> I was 18 before my mother told her sister and family members of my existence.

Rosie didn't ever meet her father; he did, however, keep in touch with Clarice and the two met up a few times, although they didn't stay together.

Clarice wrote nothing herself of her feelings for the father of her child, or even about what it would have been like to be pregnant during her final, cold few months of the war, whilst she was nursing in Belgium.

Such liaisons were commonplace throughout the war, causing untold heartbreak – even when a pregnancy did not occur. The war affected people absolutely and inescapably in so, so many ways.

I am touched that Rosie has allowed me to write this part of her mother's story, because of course it tells the story of so many. However, I think she also did so in part because she is so proud of her mother. She also wrote:

> It is difficult to realise the shame of having a child out of wedlock in those times. In the Mother and Baby Home where she stayed after my birth, she saw

the distress of other mothers handing over their babies for adoption and she couldn't do it.

She hoped she would get by somehow, which she did.

★★★

I have chosen to end Clarice Jacques' story with a mention of something she saw in the early days of the war, that – to me – represents strength and hope, because it is of a flower managing to blossom in what was otherwise a scene of terrible destruction. She wrote:

> I remember seeing the result of bomb damage in Bixley Road, in Ipswich, where one of the bungalows had been totally destroyed. In what had been the garden, a single rose defiantly poked its head through the pile of rubble, standing on a long stalk like a sentinel over the devastation.

NOTES

1 Clarice Jacques, *Travels with a Gasmask 1939–1945*, privately printed by Flexpress, Leicester, 2020
2 www.pmrafnsassociation.co.uk and en.wikipedia.org/wiki/Princess_Mary%27s_Royal_Air_Force_Nursing_Service
3 Paul Carell, 'June 6 '44 D-Day The Shock' in *Invasion! They're Coming!*, George Harrap & Co Ltd, London, 1974
4 warfarehistorynetwork.com/2019/01/11/incomplete-victory-at-malaise

GWEN RAGGETT: A WOMEN'S LAND ARMY STORY

Preparing thatching straw was not a skill Gwen Raggett (then Gwendoline Place) expected to master, or had ever even considered acquiring, at the tender age of 13½, when Prime Minister Neville Chamberlain declared Great Britain was at war with Germany on 3 September 1939. However, when the Second World War ended in Europe in May 1945, Gwen, now a young woman of 19 years, was not only proficient in thatching, but her agricultural knowledge had also expanded exponentially. She could recognise many crops which she previously barely knew existed and understood why, sometimes, they may not grow sufficiently. She also, almost instantaneously, knew the difference between a crop and a weed.

Thatching and the harvesting of crops were just two of the many vital tasks undertaken by members of the Women's Land Army (WLA)[1] during the Second World War – an army of some 200,000 young women who took the place of thousands of male farm workers who had had to leave their farms after being called up for service on the front line. Gwen Raggett was a proud and diligent member of this civilian organisation; she told me that notwithstanding countless aches and pains and/or sore eyes at the end of a long day working the land in all weathers, being a member of the WLA was 'wonderful, I loved everything about it. It was a privilege to be a part of it. I made so many friends who I've kept in touch with. I loved it all.'

Gwen was 17 when her service with the WLA began in January 1943. She was living at home in Bournemouth in Dorset at the time with her parents and youngest brother, Ron. She had two other brothers – Ted and Jack – but when they were small the family had been split up because her mother was too ill to care for them, suffering with a thyroid problem. Ted and Jack were sent to respective grandparents, and Gwen and Ron to a children's home that was run by nuns. Gwen recalled her fifth birthday, in the home, being the day she learnt to tie her shoelaces without any help! When her mother was stronger, she and Ron returned home, but Ted and Jack stayed with their grandparents.

So, when the WLA beckoned, young Gwen was ready. She had a job at a local cinema, but she happily gave it up. She was a little nervous about the way her life was about to change – completely – but at the same time was bursting with enthusiasm at the prospect of adventure. She said:

My parents were strict; most of the year I'd be in bed by 6 p.m., in the summer by 7 p.m. But I have always remembered one night when my parents woke me up quite late because the Aurora Borealis was showing in the sky, in the summer of 1939. It was rare and beautiful, but my mother said seeing it was a 'bad omen'. She was right because not long after that the war started.

My father was a barber; he had been quite ill as a child with rheumatic fever so he shouldn't have been called up. But he was, by the Army; they didn't believe my father when he said he was medically unfit and thought he was trying to skive. But he was telling the truth and he collapsed with heart problems after a couple of training parades and came home. My elder brothers couldn't serve either – my eldest brother Ted got tuberculosis in the early days of the war, which we think he contracted because of the time he spent in an air-raid shelter in Southampton; and my second brother was a plumber but had poor eyesight (he was almost blind) – so we were all at home.

As soon as I could I signed up for the Land Army. I went for an interview with a lady in Bournemouth and was accepted straightway. My parents were pleased for me that I chose to do this because they didn't want me to go into the services. I wanted, at the beginning to serve in the 'Timber Corps' (of the WLA) but they needed me in the Land Army. I didn't really mind. After being accepted I took a train, a day or so later, with a few other girls from Southampton and together we went to a lovely country mansion house near Andover, called Redenham House. When I started there were ten of us, all from the south – Southampton, Bournemouth and Portsmouth – but soon our number had grown and I was one of 100 girls living in this house. The Southampton girls (of which I was one) shared with girls from Staffordshire and London, and we all slept in dormitories on bunk beds, about eight of us in each of the large rooms, four in the smaller ones.

All the girls were about the same age as me, we looked after each other – I remember the lady who interviewed me saying I was a 'good type'; we were all 'good types' – but that doesn't mean we got things right all the time – I did disgrace myself once. I'll tell you about that later!

We were lucky because not only did we all have each other, but we also had a wonderful matron. Her name was Mrs Drake Brockman. She was strict but extremely fair. We used to talk about her after the war, we all had good memories of her. We were allowed to call her 'DB'.

I was one of the charge hands and my job was to get the girls up in the morning, waking them just before 7 a.m. The cook would come and set the 'ranges going'– then she would wake me first, then I would knock on all the doors and make sure the girls were getting up. Then we would have breakfast – we didn't go hungry, but we did have to eat whatever was available; I remember sometimes we would have cheese sandwiches and some of the girls from Staffordshire would put jam in with the cheese. The 'Southerners' – including me – thought that was rather strange – but I often have jam with cheese now! And each day we would be given a tiny bit of butter, which we had to make last because there wouldn't be any more.

Gwen, and the other ninety-nine girls at Redenham were, undoubtedly, some of the most fortunate of the WLA members (known as 'Land Girls'). Every evening, no matter how lonely/exhausted/cold/physically and mentally challenged they might have been whilst at work, they had each other for company, women together with whom they could share the ups and downs of their days, laugh and console each other. However, this camaraderie was not there for all those in the WLA – far from it; many were housed or billeted in tiny cottages with perhaps one, or two, others, some at the farms where they worked. For many it was lonely, as well as physically and mentally challenging. Gwen was more than aware of her own good fortune in this regard.

The idea of a 'Land Army' of women was first established towards the end of the First World War, in 1917, as a response to a shortage of male farmworkers, as the young men had gone off to fight, resulting in fewer people working the land – and thus, food shortages and hunger. Women were invited to step in, plug the gap and feed the nation; some 23,000 signed up to the initial WLA, which continued until it was disbanded in November 1919. In June 1939 (in expectation of the start of the Second World War) the WLA was re-formed, continuing until November 1950. The director of the reformed WLA, Lady Gertrude Denman, summed up the importance of the women's work, with the following words: 'The land army fights in the fields. It is in the fields of Britain that the most critical battle of the present war may well be fought and won.'

The purpose, reason and function for this special civilian organisation was clear, and unequivocal; the Land Girls' work was critical if food supplies were to be maintained, up and down the country, to any sort of a reasonable level. The basic working week was forty-eight hours in winter and fifty hours in the summer – sometimes working until late into the evening, just to get the work done. With little (in most cases no) experience of farming work, the Land Girls, after being accepted, often began their work with no training, honing new skills 'on the job' – ploughing, sowing, and planting seeds and crops, milking cows, catching rats, driving tractors, hoeing fields, cleaning hen houses, gathering potatoes, picking vegetables … to name but a few of their tasks. They were paid the minimum wage, which increased slightly as the war progressed. Many were attracted to it not for this meagre money, but for other reasons: an opportunity to leave home to do something different and meet new people. Also war was, of course, a time of crisis when people wanted to play 'their part'; and possibly for some girls even though it was hard graft, they would have put up with that to avoid the dangers of serving instead, perhaps in nursing, closer to the battlefield.

A government national recruitment drive, launched in the summer of 1939, invited young women from all walks of life to join the WLA, enticing them with the following words:

Join the Women's Land Army, for a Healthy Happy Job

And, in 'small print':

In the event of a war a Women's Land Army will be organised. This body will be a mobile force consisting of women who are ready to undertake all kinds of farm work in any part of the country. The members will wear uniform, although they will normally be employed and paid by individual farmers, and the organisation will supervise their lodging arrangements and their general welfare. There will also be a need for women who are only able to offer their services for work in their home district.

Signing up was initially voluntary, but this would change in December 1941, when the government ruled that some women would have to be conscripted into joining, which proved how vitally important the work of the WLA was.

In April 1940, a monthly magazine *The Land Girl* was produced for members and would-be members.[2] Designed to be as entertaining as it was informative, the following words were written by its editor Margaret Pyke in the opening article of the first edition:

There is a curious delusion that land workers are rather slower than town folk; that, like brains and brawn, cows and culture don't go together.

Perhaps it all depends on what is meant by culture. There is certainly more cash and more comfort attached to the commercial or clerical city existence. Whether it also shows a better sense of values or proves the possession of superior brains is quite another matter.

At any rate, members of the Land Army have proved their intelligence by joining the Land Army. Coming from every profession and calling, they have all realised what is the most important job they can do today.

The mention of 'intelligence' in this lovely, much needed and what proved to be extremely popular publication is interesting, and quite important. There was no escaping that almost all the work undertaken by Land Girls was manual, because its primary purpose was to gather food. It was, by a huge margin, hard, physical, repetitive graft – be that graft the collection of potatoes (in their hundreds) thrown up by a tractor, sweeping out and dousing down hen houses and/or pig styes, picking brussels sprouts off their stalks (again in their hundreds), or thrashing corn. All of this work needed to be done, no matter the weather or how tired the 'Girls' might be.

However, there was a need for wit, intelligence, and perhaps most importantly common sense. Land Girls were often tasked with huge responsibilities, requiring knowledge they had to simply gather 'on the job', including the management of such things as farm machinery, but also – in Gwen's case –

vehicles. Gwen was the nominated 'taxi' driver for many of the other girls. She drove a 3-tonne lorry during much of her service. She said:

One of my jobs, at the beginning and the end of each day was to drive a bunch of Redenham girls to and from their farms each day, in a great big lorry. It wasn't just a case of doing the driving, I had to look after it too – we weren't allowed to change the tyres, so I'd go to a garage if I had a problem with those, but I had to do everything else – including putting water in the engine every day, and I learnt how to demobilise it by taking out the rotor arm. But I do remember the brakes on the lorry worked very well – almost too well – the girls sat on benches at the back and if I had to brake suddenly, the girls would thrown forward and bang against the back of the cab …

In the winter when the screen was frozen – which happened a lot – I would scrape the ice away with half a potato. It really worked!

One of the trickiest journeys I had driving the lorry was at the end of a day when I'd been rather naughty … I was doing a thatching job with another girl and we sneaked off to a pub at lunchtime. I drank too much cider – not realising how strong it was – so not only could I not get up the ladder when I went back in the afternoon, I was probably too tipsy to drive the lorry. But I got away with it!

Gwen Raggett MBE, in 1943.

Gwen also mentioned that quite often they would be instructed to share their duties on the farms with Prisoners of War (POWs); in her case (and in the case of most of her friends at Redenham) these were German and Italian POWs.

At the beginning of the war, Britain accommodated very few POWs because government policy was to send them to Canada. This was for two reasons: fewer mouths to feed at a time when supplies were low, and the further they were from Germany the harder it was for them to rejoin their home army if they managed to escape. It wasn't until the last few months of the war – particularly following D-Day (6 June 1944) – that numbers of prisoners of war held in the United Kingdom suddenly increased substantially. The British and American governments decided after D-Day that the Axis captives would be split equally between the United States and the United Kingdom, the decisive factor being the initial letter of their surname – those who belonged to the beginning of the alphabet 'crossed the pond' – and vice versa!

So, POWs with names starting between M and Z would have been those Gwen met and worked with. They were probably housed at one of around seventeen camps that sprang up in Hampshire alone. Not complaining at all about the prisoners, she said they often brightened her day, and their very presence gave the girls plenty to talk about in the evenings. She said:

> We weren't really allowed to work alongside the prisoners. Usually, they would be at one end of the field, and I would be at the other. Sometimes they were the lucky ones – I remember now, if the weather was dreadful, they didn't have to keep working, but we did. We had to do things like pick Brussels sprouts in freezing cold weather, and we didn't even have gloves.
>
> The Italians were the most entertaining – but they could be really annoying too. More than once when I was tasked with cleaning out hen and chicken huts the Italian POWs working at the farm tried to distract me by singing love songs – I remember having to lock myself into a shed to get them to stop!

However, friendships did – inevitably and happily – develop between some of the prisoners and the Land Girls, and Gwen mentioned that one of the girls at Redenham ended up marrying a German soldier.

By December 1945 (six months after the end of the war) over 200,000 German and Italian prisoners were still being held in the UK, many of whom were employed on farms because the need for them was still very great.

The need for the WLA remained too, and it continued until it was disbanded in 1950. The WLA hit its peak in 1943, employing over 80,000 girls – Gwen was one of many, however, who remained loyal for almost as long as she could – she didn't leave until November 1949, four months after she got married. Gwen said:

> I am sure my years as a Land Girl set me up for my long and happy marriage to Maurice – we were married for 68 years, until he died in 2018. I met my husband at Church – we were childhood sweethearts. He was a choir boy; he would follow me home after the service. We didn't see very much of each other during the war because he was in the Merchant Navy and spent much of the time travelling to New Zealand and Australia, but we kept in touch by letter, and married just a few weeks before I stopped being a Land Girl.

Falling in love, getting married and contemplating motherhood would almost certainly been on the minds of many of the Land Girls throughout their service – in those days women did marry and start families much younger – and these girls were mostly in their late teens or early twenties. The presence of American servicemen, for many of the Land Girls, was therefore a welcome and much-needed distraction to the routine and drudgery of daily work:

> We had great fun with some of the American, and Canadian, servicemen. We'd occasionally see them at the end of our working days driving or walking around – they were really kind and would share delicious things with us like steak sandwiches or sweets (they had treats whereas we didn't!) but mostly we'd meet up with them on the occasional Saturday evening, at dances that would take place at local RAF and Army bases, in Tidworth near Ludgershall or Andover. Some of the girls became G.I. brides.
>
> But we also made our own fun! Back at Redenham we had our own mini-theatre – we would put on plays, mostly for ourselves but sometimes we'd invite some of the G.I.'s to watch. I remember, particularly, in 1946 we put on 'Babes in the Wood' (a fairy tale about a brother and sister left in the care of an uncle and aunt after their parent's death. It can be adapted in whatever way a producer wishes). I played Maid Marian in our production, and we took it to show local people in different villages. We raised money for the North and South Tidworth Welcome Home Fund.

The G.I.'s could be a bit naughty though. During the day whilst out in the field if you needed to 'spend a penny' you had to just get on with it. I remember doing this once and an American plane flew over, quite low, and before I could get up, he came back!

Gwen Raggett certainly reflected upon her service with, most of all, gratitude that she was able to be of service to the country in such a way that she was distanced from much of the danger of war; but mostly she is grateful for the friendships she developed. Most of her WLA friends have died now, Gwen told me, but she stayed in touch with many throughout her life, meeting up at Butlins holiday camps and at other reunions. One of the most special of their Remembrance events took place in 1990 at Redenham House, when Gwen planted a tree in memory of all who served in the WLA. The tree, she said, was given to her by Sir John Marshall, who has lived there for over thirty years; there is also a plaque, which Gwen provided herself.

Her experience in the WLA instilled in her a long life of service. Between 1964 and 2020 Gwen served in the Royal Voluntary Service, which she found immensely rewarding not only for the care she was able to provide, but for the opportunity it gave her to meet local people; she received an MBE in 2005 for her loyalty and dedication.

Unsurprisingly, given her humility, Gwen said of this reward: 'It as a lovely surprise to get this, but it wasn't really just for me, it was for lots of people because we are a team. I don't really see why I should have it!'

However, I think I would be doing Gwen, and indeed the thousands of other Land Girls, a disservice if I did not reflect on some of the tougher memories Gwen drew to my attention. Exhaustion, aches and pains, and homesickness were, for many Land Girls, often the order of the day. Gwen said:

The potato work was really hard. We all suffered having to do that – we would have a big basket which would have to push along whilst on all fours picking up potatoes thrown up by a tractor in front of us. We'd get backache. Matron (DB) was really kind and gave us aspirin, but never a day off unless we were really ill. We'd have to just get on with it.

Thrashing corn was awful too. Lots of dust would be thrown up, clouds of it, and because we didn't have protective goggles or anything the dust would make our eyes extremely sore. I hated that, and it was especially hard driving the lorry with sore eyes too.

I don't know which was worse – driving rain or relentless heat. That was when I got into trouble – I was thatching in a field once when it was really hot, there was no-one around so I took my shirt off and tied my scarf around me. But the farmer took a photograph of me, which ended up in a local newspaper, and the lady who had interviewed me saw it and drove all the way to Redenham to give me a ticking-off!

Gwen acknowledged, too, how fortunate she felt that in their part of Hampshire they were quite sheltered from the immediate dangers of war; but that was not the case, of course, for all Land Girls. Many served in parts of the country closer to towns and cities and those women, even if rarely directly, would have felt far more the impact of, for example, the Blitz – seeing, hearing and fearing the enemy aircraft that would have flown directly over them.

Also – and I should point out that this is not something Gwen drew to my attention because she is not someone who I think would want to be seen as 'complaining' about anything – there is an injustice that needs to be mentioned: the simple fact that WLA members were paid less than their male counterparts for doing the same work. It wasn't until 1943 that a 'Land Girls Charter' was introduced that stipulated Land Girls must have a week's holiday a year, and the occasional long weekend off. Towards the end of the war a decision was taken in Parliament that Land Girls were to be excluded from post-war benefits such as capital grants to restart businesses, post-war education, and the right to reclaim pre-war jobs – the justification being they were 'auxiliaries to industry'. Lady Denham resigned as a director in protest, but at least a Land Army Benevolent Fund was set up for women in the greatest need to draw from, and they were allowed to keep parts of their uniform. The women and their families could also apply to receive a special veteran's badge from 2007.

Conversely, something that was special, priceless and can never be taken away, were the letters (each one personalised with their names and dates of service) sent to every Land Girl by the Patron of the WLA Queen Elizabeth (consort of George VI), shortly after the war ended:

By this message I wish to express to you my appreciation of your loyal and devoted service as a member of the Women's Land Army. Your unsparing efforts at a time when the victory of our cause depended on the utmost use of the resources of our land have earned for you the country's gratitude.

★★★

Many poems and songs have been written by Land Girls, sung during the war years and for years after to strengthen, cheer and raise sometimes beleaguered and exhausted spirits. Below are the words of the best-known, called 'Back to the Land':

Back to the Land, we must all lend a hand,
To the farms and the fields we must go.
There's a job to be done,
Though we can't fire a gun,
We can still do our bit with the hoe.

When your muscles are strong
You will soon get along,
And you'll think a country life's grant.
We're all needed now,
We must speed to the plough,
So come with us – back to the Land.

NOTES

1 www.womenslandarmy.co.uk
2 womenslandarmy.co.uk/running-the-wla-the-land-girl-magazine

MARY WILSON: A LADY ALMONER MEMORY

As Mary Wilson began to talk to me about her memories of the Second World War, I suddenly noticed a cheerful, smiling photograph of Queen Elizabeth II on a mantlepiece over the fireplace of her cosy sitting room, in which we were seated. I knew that Mary had had her 100th birthday in 2020 and the photograph, on her centenary birthday card, served as a useful reminder to me of Mary's great age. I realised as soon as I met her that I could not possibly write about her as 100 years 'old', but 100 years 'young'. For much of the time Mary spoke faster than I could write, recollections flowing like water from a tap, as though the war ended only yesterday … it was a truly fascinating and engaging conversation. This is the story of Mary Wilson, from Sudbury in Suffolk; 100 Years Young.

★★★

At 19 years old when war was declared in September 1939, Mary Wilson (née Dawson) initially had her heart set on becoming a Land Girl. She wanted to be useful, and a national recruitment drive was calling for girls of her age to sign up – so it seemed the obvious thing to do. But also, she admitted, 'it sounded like it would be fun' – and I did think to myself that I probably would have felt the same if I had been in her position. However, a countryside placement as a Land Girl was not to be for Mary, because she was very bright and her parents persuaded her that she would be more useful, eventually, to the country if she were to carry on with her education. So this is what she did – and shortly after Neville Chamberlain's announcement that Britain was at war with Germany, Mary Wilson began a two-year social work diploma at the London School of

Economics (LSE). The diploma she received enabled her, two years later, to reach out and help many hundreds of very needy children and families in a way she would never have expected before her LSE studies began.

Mary's place of study, despite still being known as the 'London' School of Economics, was not actually in London; because of the potential dangers of war it was evacuated to Cambridge. Mary said that when she learned she would be moving out of London to a city as lovely as Cambridge she couldn't have been more delighted. It was a relief for her parents too that she was to spend at least the beginning of the war in a place of relative safety. Mary was the youngest of four siblings – both her elder brothers, Philip and Jack, were fit enough for service and her sister, Katharine, was already working by the start of the war as a radiographer at the Passmore Edwards Hospital in north London.

Philip, the eldest in the family, had been in the RAF for some years before the war, and Jack was called up immediately because he was already signed up in the Territorial Army, under the Honourable Artillery Company. Jack remained in England for most of the war, but at the beginning of 1944, whilst it was still occupied, he was sent to France. But within a day, Mary said:

Poor Jack was ambushed and taken prisoner the day after he arrived in France. To this day I remember my mother's face when we received a telegram to say he was missing. She was so distressed she couldn't cope in London and went to Somerset to stay with her brother. Amazingly, however, news reached us before long that Jack was at least safe; albeit in a POW camp in Germany. We learned after the war that Jack was taken within a day of arriving in Maltot, in the Normandy region of France. But I can still remember the day he came home … he was like a skeleton, he was so thin. I can't say much more because Jack would never talk about it. We learned afterwards that within a day of arriving in Maltot in France Jack was captured and imprisoned at a POW camp in Germany.

Philip worked in management for the RAF – as a career officer deploying staff and organising men, and aircraft. I am surprised he chose the RAF because Philip didn't have very good eyesight, so he was never going to be a pilot or a navigator. He had quite a 'good war', I think, behind the scenes. I remember that two of the places he was posted to were Crete and Habbinayah in Iraq, but it was hard too, involving lots of trekking and travelling. I can't quite remember when he was at both places – but for quite a long time each, I think.

Crete, together with the rest of the Greek islands, was occupied for most of the war, falling into Nazi hands in the spring of 1941. RAF Habbinayah, which was situated on the west bank of the enormous Euphrates river, was relatively peaceful, serving as the location of an important flying training school, and later in the war as a base for several operational RAF squadrons; I imagine there was rarely a dull or quiet moment, with lots of aircraft – and their crews – passing through. It was only during the month of May in 1941 that fierce fighting was seen at RAF Habbinayah, because it fell under attack by units from the Royal Iraqi Army. The month-long battle became known as the Anglo-Iraqi War, which the Allies won but with losses of around 200 men and over 20 aircraft.

However, we return now to the United Kingdom and Cambridge, where Mary Wilson's Second World War began. To be precise, as this is written in the spring of 2021, the autumn of 1939 is exactly eighty-one and a half years ago; a lifetime for most of us, but a mere moment in the history of this fine city. The university for which it is most famous, with its thirty-one colleges, dates back to 1209, but less well known is that it was an important trading centre during the Roman and Viking ages, too, and there is even archaeological evidence of settlement in the area as early as the Bronze Age. But let's not worry too much about the battles and fights that may have been happening in Cambridge some 4,000 years ago; let us fast-forward to the dates in which we are interested: September 1939 until the summer of 1941, which was the time during the war Mary Wilson resided in Cambridge, resplendent with its spires and scenic views over the River Cam.

Cambridge is only about 60 miles from the centre of London; but with the Essex countryside protecting it from the capital city, in many respects it feels it could be a much further distance. It did not, therefore, feel the impact of the Battle of Britain from July to September in 1940; but it was attacked during the Blitz that followed, which saw the Germans, in retribution for their defeat in the Battle of Britain, dropping bombs over many cities in the United Kingdom until May the following year. Around thirty people lost their lives during air attacks on the city, many more were badly hurt and about fifty houses were completely destroyed. The worst night of loss of life for Cambridge during the war was 24 February 1941; eleven people were killed following the dropping of many incendiary bombs near the Grantchester Meadow area of the city from German Heinkel aircraft, which were one of the Luftwaffe's most used medium-range bombers.

Mary was fortunate to have been in the 'right place at the right time' whilst in Cambridge; of course, the time and place of dying for all of us is an unknown we all live with, wartime or not, but during war the possibility of an untimely death is, inevitably, greater. But Mary, with youth on her side, did not – it seemed from the way she related her memories to me – allow such fears to impinge on her enjoyment. She said:

There was magic in the air in Cambridge in those days. We would cycle everywhere and felt safe. At night, the only light would be from the moon, and it would light up the colleges and they looked so beautiful. Cambridge wasn't bombed very much, either; I can only remember once an explosion happening just down the road from where I was having supper one evening, and my friends and I diving under the table.

Mary Wilson punting along the Cam, *c.* 1939.

Other magical moments Mary recalled were musical. Music, she said, has been very important to her throughout her whole life (I wonder if it has aided her longevity?). She said:

> Being at Cambridge gave me the opportunity to join the Cambridge University Musical Society, and I was able to sing in places such as King's College Chapel, and Ely Cathedral. The most amazing piece of music I remember singing was Beethoven's 'Missa Solemnis' at King's. It was wonderful, I've never forgotten it.

In the course of my research for Mary's story it would have been neglectful if I didn't listen to this myself. I am so glad I did. I also discovered that at the head of the autograph score of 'Missa Solemnis', Beethoven inscribed the words, 'from the heart – may it return again – to the heart.' Being completely 'unmusical' I don't feel qualified to say much more, except that I completely agree with Mary that it is an amazing piece, and it was heart-warming, too, to think of beautiful music being performed, and bringing comfort to performers and audience alike, during such a frightening time as the war was.

However, moonlight and music aside, Mary's two years of study for her diploma were far from easy. She did have youth on her side, and a positive spirit, but much to learn too – driven on, I expect, by the thought of not only a proper salary to follow but also – perhaps more importantly – a need to serve during such a crucial time. I was surprised by one of the most long-lasting memories Mary recalled – that of being very cold! She said:

> My first billet was with a wonderful old lady who lived in a large Victorian house near St Paul's Church. Two other students were there with me, as well as a maid. My bedroom stuck out at the back – so it had three outside walls – it was a really cold winter, and I would wake up in the morning with icicles on my blanket, and my water jug being full of ice! But that said, I am lucky, I had a wonderful time – and after the two years, I did receive my diploma.

It was in the summer of 1941, as her time at Cambridge came to an end, that Mary Wilson decided to train to be a hospital lady almoner.[1] This role can best be described as a 'medical social worker' – an important job during the war because it was the responsibility of the almoners to assess patients who came to them; the doctors would assess their medical needs and the almoners would then assess the individual family's potential ability to fund even a proportion of their care. This was Mary's position at the Great Ormond Street Children's Hospital in central London for the last three years of the war.

In between her studies in Cambridge and becoming an almoner in London, however, Mary had to complete a year-long training course. She was given the option of completing her almoner traineeship at St Thomas's Hospital in London or at various hospitals around the country, and – being young and adventurous – chose the latter. Her placements were at hospitals in cities including Manchester, Bristol and St Albans – around six weeks in each location. Mary described these placements as 'very interesting' in different ways, and they certainly prepared her extremely well for the almoner work she was eventually paid for at Great Ormond Street. But, although Mary did not complain at all, it must have been hard, being so young, to travel to different places – especially during wartime – and to see so many families in considerable distress and difficulty because of the challenges that the war was presenting them. Of Bristol, one of her first placements, she recalled:

> When I arrived here, my first job was to find myself somewhere to stay. I went to some 'digs' I had been recommended, but they were awful. Just a tiny room in a concrete block, that was little more than a cell, with a hard bed and a little table. It was then known as 'settlement accommodation', similar to those in the East End of London, run by colleges. So I gave that up for a 'game of soldiers' and quickly found myself a much more comfortable room in the Old Assembly Rooms, where I shared a room with a friend. I worked at the Bristol Royal Infirmary. There was so much to do, it was very hard; so much of the centre of Bristol had been bombed by that point.

Bristol was a key target area for the Germans – in part because of its shipyards and harbour, and the aircraft factories in which planes such as Bristol Blenheims and Beaufighters were manufactured. Bombs were dropped on the city quite regularly throughout most of the war, but most heavily during the 'Bristol Blitz', which began at the end of November in 1940 and ended at the end of April 1941. So, by the time Mary arrived, the city would have been a shadow of its former self. The hospital itself escaped heavy bombing – only its mortuary was destroyed – but it was a 'Casualty Receiving Hospital', and, therefore, Mary's work there was, she reported, at times 'distressing, and eye-opening'.

Mary eventually began her work as a lady almoner at Great Ormond Street Hospital in London in the summer of 1942. She worked with two other 'lady almoners', each of whom had a different area of responsibility. Mary's job, as the Medical Outpatient's Lady Almoner, was to talk to the parents (usually mothers, as fathers were often away) to establish if they could afford to pay anything towards care, after their child or children had been medically assessed. This was of course extremely important: the National Health Service had not, by this point, been established (it was founded in 1948), so hospitals had to fundraise to survive. At that time they were mostly funded by generous endowment payments, but this was rarely a reliable or regular source of income. She said:

> I did enjoy this work, I think because I was so busy I really felt I was doing something useful, and we worked well as a team. Sometimes I would arrive at work in the morning, at about 9 a.m. A long queue of families would build up during the morning, all wanting to be seen. Sometimes there would be up to sixty children. Fortunately, most of the parents were quite upfront about whether they could afford to pay anything – in those days you had to just trust people. Very often you simply knew people couldn't pay, and I wouldn't press them. How could I push an exhausted mother who looked very poor and had travelled for miles with a very sick child, who hadn't seen her husband for weeks, and didn't even know if she would see him again?
>
> My office was in an old part of the hospital, just above the chapel built in the Victorian era, but adjacent to it was a new state-of-the-art hospital. Occasionally we would see a rat (or two!). One scuttled across the attic above me one day and fell off the top of a door on to the floor in front of me!
>
> There was never a dull moment – one of my great friends was the girl who was the Surgical Lady Almoner – sometimes we would have a giggle about the children's names, because it was my job to call them out. I remember particularly 'Stuart Amato' and 'Theresa Greene' ('stew a tomato', and 'trees are green')!

I am sure a sense of humour was essential to be able to cope with the trauma of seeing so many children every day, many of whom were suffering very much indeed. Part of Mary's job, too, in common with the other lady almoners, was to establish if they considered the parents who brought a child in were able to continue caring for the child, or if they might have been neglecting the child, in which case more thorough assessment was done and occasionally a child would be taken away from them.

The war, inevitably, affected the health of all the population, especially children. First and foremost, their mental health suffered; many had to become 'adults' from an early age, helping out with manual tasks that absent fathers or brothers would have done in the home or on the farm. In addition, over 10 per cent of children of the patients were evacuees, most of whom would have needed special support to deal with the separation from their homes and families. And of course, sadly, many children would have been bereaved and would have had that to cope with too.

Aside from children the lady almoners attended to, who had clear physical injuries, the most common health problems that they saw in children included head lice, skin diseases and poor nutrition because of food rationing. Rationing was carefully worked out and young people were rationed more eggs and milk than adults because of the calcium contained in these foods that is vital for growth, but most children simply did not get enough, the result being a prevalence of rickets – weak bone disease caused by a vitamin D deficiency. There was, however, a surplus of some foods – carrots being one! In 1941 the Ministry of Food created a character called 'Dr Carrot, The Children's Best Friend' – a lively-looking 'carrot cartoon chap' who wore a top hat and tails. Through Dr Carrot, different carrot recipes were issued by the Ministry to families up and down the country: carrot jam, carrot lollies, carrot curry and even carrot pudding.[2]

Mary's work at the hospital was clearly exacting, requiring her to make difficult decisions on a regular basis, but it was also fulfilling, as she saw many young lives made so much happier, and more comfortable, because of the help the hospital was able to provide. Mary spoke about how well she and her colleagues worked together, looking after each other when they were upset or not very well. She recalled:

During my first year I kept getting ill, which was very annoying; I got measles, mumps, tonsilitis and jaundice – each time I thought I would lose my job, but my boss kindly didn't lose patience and took me back, thank goodness. There was also another day I remember arriving at work and bursting into tears because the night before there had been an explosion at the end of our road. A lovely old lady I knew quite well died, which made me really sad, and I remember being very tired that day too because I had stayed up most of the night making tea and giving it to firemen helping clear up the mess, and to the neighbours.

Often, too, the end of her day in her office as a lady almoner did not mark the end of her working day; they were expected to help, sometimes, with other duties, such as fire-watching.

'We would be a paid 3s 6d an evening for doing this,' Mary said:

It basically meant we had to sit and look out of a high window on the top floor of the nurses home and look out for any bombs or fires that might appear. It was on one of these shifts that I did see a bomb, once – a 'buzz bomb'. It was really frightening. I could see it and hear it coming down; it was falling very fast and was really noisy. It landed nearby in Russell Square, I don't think that bomb hurt anyone, but it was horrible. I have never run down the stairs so fast (to tell people about it) in all my life.

★★★

During the three years Mary worked at Great Ormond Street she lived back at the family home in Highgate, which she particularly enjoyed because her elder sister, Katharine, also lived there. She told me how pleased they were to be back together after Mary's time away in Cambridge and her almoner training around the country:

Katharine also worked in a hospital, at the Passmore Edwards in north London, so in the evenings we would have plenty of stories to swap and lots to talk about. She was ten years older than me and worked as a radiographer – one of the first women to train to do this, in the 1920s. After the war Katharine sadly lost two babies, probably because of the radiation but it wasn't known then that being around x-rays all the time could affect a woman's fertility. But she did have a healthy baby girl eventually, which made us all very happy.

Sometimes in the evenings, after our work at our hospitals we would meet up and help serve meals at canteens, volunteering with service men's clubs, usually giving food to Canadians on duty in London. This was fun and quite a laugh after a stressful day.

At home, my father had arranged for our air-raid shelter to be put in the kitchen, rather than the garden. (I don't quite know why but I am glad he did because I've heard so many stories about how cold people got in their shelters in the garden). The shelter was really a big metal cage, with mesh sides and a solid metal top. It was big enough for us both to sleep in, so we did quite often; but one night we were suddenly woken up by a loud scratching noise and we saw lots of cockroaches scaling up the outside of the cage – after that we only went back in when the siren sounded and we absolutely had to! And that was the last time we ever slept in it, too.

Finally, Mary told me she felt a chapter written about her Second World War memories would be incomplete without a mention of food. She was lucky, she told me, because her mother was a 'clever and imaginative' cook and would usually be able to make something quite healthy and tasty out of the most meagre of rations. She recalled how special Christmas was during the war, as this was a time they would be given a few extra 'morsels' of dried fruit or chocolate. She said, 'It is hard to imagine now just how much we appreciated these small, extra Christmas treats – we simply didn't have them for the rest of the year.'

However, something Mary Wilson certainly won't be eating again, the dreadful taste of which she can still remember (and echoing Dorothy Drew's sentiments too): whale meat. She told me she had it once and would rather starve than eat it again: 'It was so disgusting!' Its 'awfulness' was closely followed by another wartime staple, 'Woolton Pie', which was a root vegetable pie made with pastry that 'tasted like wood', Mary said. It was so called because it was named after Lord Woolton, the Minister of Food. Mary said, 'I've no doubt Lord Woolton did his best, and he had a difficult job. But if anyone offers me Woolton Pie again, I shall say a very firm "no thank you!"'

NOTES

1 hharp.org/library/gosh/general/hospital-almoner.html
2 www.carrotmuseum.co.uk

PART 2:

MEMORIES FROM AROUND THE WORLD

YOKA VERDONER:
THE STORY OF A DUTCH
CHILD IN HIDING

The delicate white petals of Yoka Verdoner's cyclamen blew gently in the chilly autumn breeze. It was September 1942; her home country of the Netherlands had been in the grip of German occupation for over a year and Yoka's family, being Jewish, were learning to live with the fear of separation and possible death daily. Yoka, then, was only 7½ years old – too young to understand why the world around her had become so different, but old enough to know that what was happening felt very wrong and very frightening.

Perhaps that is why she delighted so much in the small white flower, which she loved for its simple beauty. However, the purity of its whiteness represented peace; something even a 7-year-old child, if subconsciously, longed for. What child would not have wanted their world to be as it was before the war, when children could safely play outside with their friends, go shopping with their parents and sleep at night without fear that their mother or father might not be there in the morning?

So, when Yoka's parents decided in September 1942 that, for her own protection, she, and both her younger brother Otto and sister Francisca, must go to into hiding, the cyclamen was one of two possessions that she took with her. The other was a splendid two-tiered bookshelf made of blond wood. Yoka recalled that, even as a young girl, 'I already loved both books and plants.'

The first of several hiding places Yoka stayed in was a children's home run by two elderly ladies, who took in Jewish children even though it was illegal for them to do so. The home was called Zonneschijn, meaning 'sunshine', and it was located in a small town called Zeist, about an hour's drive from their home. Yoka told me she did not recall feeling unhappy there, that she got on well with the other children and had plenty to eat – but that it was cold most of the time. She does, however, have quite clear memories of her mother's visits to see her at this home, not least because these were the last times she saw her. In early 1943 Yoka's mother was deported to Auschwitz, never to return. Yoka recalled:

> My mother would occasionally make the two-hour bicycle trip from Amsterdam, where all Dutch Jews had been forced to relocate, to Zeist to visit me. I particularly remember one such visit. I was sitting in the child seat behind my mother on her bicycle as we were going to visit some friends in that neighbourhood. My mother wore a dark long-haired fur coat, and I was stroking the fur, admiring the way it turned darker or lighter as I stroked it up and down.

Yoka spent around three months at Zonneschijn, after which she was moved with the same speed at which she had been sent there – her father had heard it was going to be raided. He managed to arrange for her to be quickly transferred to stay at the family home of some German Jewish friends of theirs called the Meyers, who – thankfully for Yoka – had two daughters close to her in age. This couple did not need to hide themselves because Leni Meyer (the wife) was not Jewish by birth, so the Germans considered them a mixed couple; nevertheless, they took a risk taking in Yoka and she was only there for a short time. However, it was whilst she was here that Yoka had her eighth birthday, the day she last saw her mother. She said: 'My mother came for my birthday, again cycling all the way from Amsterdam. I still have the book she gave me, which is inscribed, "For my dear Yoka, sweetheart, from MAMA."'

There is a certain irony that it was her mother who died during the war years, not her father. Yoka told me that before she was sent away there was disagreement between them about what should happen – her mother was in a constant state of denial about what was happening, believing the war couldn't last and it would all be 'alright', whereas her father was more of a realist, acknowledging the danger they were in and their need to hide.

★★★

The tearing apart of families was a devastating weapon of war inflicted upon millions of Jews across Europe during the war. Children, if they survived, were forever shaped by the fact their own family unit was destroyed; in the case of the Verdoner family, for three years these three very young children did not see each other or their father, and none, after the war, ever saw their mother again. Also, their father, as you will read later, was a changed man, too, because of his war experience and the loss of his wife and parents. The Verdoner children's experience of grief and separation was commonplace amongst Jewish families across Europe.

The true Second World World War story of the Verdoner children is one of survival, even though that survival meant that all three children have borne psychological scars for the rest of their lives. However, many European Jewish children did not survive. Out of the 6 million European Jews who died in Nazi gas chambers, around 1.5 million were children.[1] It was not until after the war, after the Nazis were defeated, that the staggering human toll of the Holocaust began to be understood, when the number of children who died also became clear. When Auschwitz was liberated in late January 1945, only 451 Jewish children were discovered amongst the 9,000 prisoners who survived.[2]

In the early days of the war, the Jewish population in the Netherlands numbered around 140,000; by the end of the war about 105,000 had been killed in Nazi gas chambers, children as well as adults. The persecution of the Dutch people – Jews and Gentiles – by the Nazis began in 1942, two years after the country became occupied in May 1940. By this point, the heart of Rotterdam (the Netherlands' second largest city) had been very badly bombed, the government and the royal family had fled, and anti-Jewish measures were almost immediately put in place, initially banning them from public places. It was not long before the persecution became much more severe; by the summer of 1942 the first of thousands of Dutch Jews were sent to concentration camps.[3]

There was an attempted rebellion by the Dutch – both Jewish and non-Jewish – in February 1941; they organised what became known as the 'February Strike' in response to German forces raiding the Jewish Quarter in Amsterdam, and the arrest and deportation of over 400 men. This was a brave act and unique in Nazi-occupied Europe, but sadly it achieved very little – in fact it proved counter-productive, because many of the Jews living in the Jewish Quarter in the capital were sent to concentration camps.

Later in the war, in early 1944, thousands of non-Jewish young Dutch men were sent to Germany to undertake hard labour in factories, as part of a work programme called Arbeitseinsatz. It was dangerous work, not least because many of the factories they were subjected to working in were bomb-production centres or places for war manufacturing – thus targets for the Allies.

A few months later, beginning in November 1944, many Dutch people suffered with a hardship of another type: hunger. A famine began to take hold in heavily populated and Nazi-occupied parts of western Netherlands, including in the cities of The Hague, Amsterdam, and Rotterdam.[4] The Allies had been able to liberate most of the south of the country, but efforts to liberate further north were halted because they had suffered a defeat, in September 1944, when they tried to gain control of the bridge across the Rhine at Arnhem (known as the Battle of Arnhem). Following this defeat, the Dutch government, on the request of the Allied Command

and the resistance, imposed a national railway strike with the idea that this would assist the Allied liberation efforts, but in response Germany placed an embargo on all shipping carrying food to the people in the west of the Netherlands, at the same time requisitioning food for themselves. The decision to lift the shipping embargo had been taken in October 1944, but the railway strike continued; the Dutch Prime Minister broadcast that if the trains started running again they would be attacked by the Allied air force. Food did start to arrive by ship, but to make matters worse it was an extremely cold, harsh winter, and canals and waterways froze, blocking transportation routes. Food such as butter, bread and cheese depleted in supply as the famine progressed, resulting in many people eating sugar beet and tulip bulbs to survive. Fuel supplies were cut too, so people were unable to heat their homes.

The famine – which become known as *Hongerwinter* – continued until the Netherlands was liberated in May 1945, resulted in the deaths of some 22,000 Dutch (mostly men) and also caused serious health issues for some 4.5 million, including thousands of children, who, because of the malnourishment, have grown up with conditions such as coeliac disease, rickets and anaemia, to name but a few. As a response to *Hongerwinter*, a rescue operation called Operation Manna was implemented by the Allies – with the permission of the German army – during which aircrews dropped food parcels from aircraft. The cruel famine was the result of multiple factors caused by actions and responses in both the Allied and German war efforts.

However, returning to the Netherlands' Jewish population – which included Yoka and her family – whilst it sadly failed to save the vast majority of the country's Jews, the Netherlands had a resistance (or underground) movement consisting of scattered groups of members, who did manage to save thousands of Jews. The hundreds of men and women who joined this movement risked their lives to protect hundreds of others. Their hatred of the Nazis' cruelty was matched only by the Nazis' hatred of them. The resistance consisted of civilians who carried out their work in several different guises. They were involved in acts of sabotage (cutting telephone lines and distributing anti-Nazi propaganda), spying and hiding Jews, including many children. In early 1944, some 4,500 Jewish Dutch children had been displaced from their families to a place of safety, mostly by resistance members.

After the war, the Dutch government expressed its gratitude to members of the resistance who had taken the greatest risks for others with the announcement of an award called the Verzetskruis (Resistance Cross) 1940–1945. It is the second-highest medal in the Netherlands given for bravery; of the ninety-five people awarded it, ninety-three died during the war. However, for many years after the war, life in the Netherlands was hard for Jews who did return from concentration camps. Many of them were homeless because whilst they were away people had moved into their homes. Few had jobs to return to and those who had businesses (like Yoka's father) had seen them taken over. Many company directors did not re-employ their staff or were unwilling to re-establish the ownership structure that had previously existed. Also, the Dutch government imposed all kinds of rules and regulations, and even fined Jewish returnees for not paying taxes during the war – not taking into account that the reason they were unable to pay was because they were incarcerated.

The impact of all the above was felt by all, including children – Jewish or Gentile – countrywide. The effect on the health and well-being of thou-

sands of children, both during the war and in the longer term, was irrefutable – not to mention the grieving at such a young age, with so many losing parents, brothers, sisters, grandparents, friends and their homes. When I first spoke to Yoka about her story for this book, she told me she was a little concerned her story 'might not have enough drama'. I explained to her that this book is not about 'drama', it is about reality. The loss and separation she experienced

Yoka Verdoner, aged 8, holding her younger sister Francisca.

was sadly commonplace for so many. Yoka is telling their story too. Far from not having 'enough drama', I wish there were not so much. As much as I am committed to writing about the Second World War, I am so sorry there is so much to write because so much happened. However, because these things happened, they must be told; only through the truth can we understand the Second World War, and by understanding hopefully future generations might be able to prevent such atrocities happening again.

★★★

Yoka's salvation during the Second World War, and that of Otto and Francisca, was thanks to the courage of ordinary Dutch citizens who took them into their homes. It was not for some years after the war had ended that she began to truly appreciate the risks these different family members took in hiding all three of them, and how 'lucky' they were.

'We owe our survival,' she said 'to our father too. It was thanks to his foresight in insisting we go into hiding, when my mother had not yet fully grasped the seriousness of the danger we were all in.'

Yoka stayed in two more homes after leaving the Meyer family at the end of 1942. Both were formative and memorable, for different reasons.

Her next hiding address was short-lived and not the happiest time for her. During this brief interlude, whilst longer-term arrangements were made for her, she stayed with a couple called Grada and Hans van de Beek – Grada had been her mother's helper before the war; they had only married recently and were expecting their first child. Yoka told me:

Hans was a member of the Marechaussee (Dutch) police force as well as the resistance, although I was unaware of the latter. They lived in a small apartment in The Hague and agreed to take me in while a new address was being searched for. It was urgent, because their next-door neighbour was known to be a collaborator, a member of the Dutch Nazi Party. In addition, because Grada was pregnant she was not feeling well, and I was not a model child. Grada was not great at handling children, and I talked back and was no doubt uncooperative. It was not happy combination for either of us. I remember Hans coming home one evening and giving me a lecture about improving my behaviour. I respected Hans and knew he was right.

It was after this, in January 1943, that Yoka arrived at the home she stayed in until the war was over. Whilst it could not ever be a place she genuinely wanted to be because of the circumstances of why she was there, it was, she said, as close to giving her an 'ideal childhood' as anything could have done.

This family home was in a small farming village called Woubrugge, which was about 20 miles north-east of The Hague, in the west of the Netherlands. The house, called Jacobswoude (meaning Jacob's Wood), was the official residence of the mayor of Woubrugge, Dirk Rijnders, who lived there with his wife Ella Rijnders van Kempen. Yoka recalled her memories of arriving at Jacobswoude, which proved to be a loving home for her. She said:

A long, graceful driveway led to a large, beautiful house with a traditional straw roof right next to a wide waterway. The peaceful setting belied the reality of what was happening in the Netherlands in January of 1943. I was brought there early that month and would be staying for about two and a half years. Dirk and Ella were both 34 years old. Ella had soft brown eyes and a warm voice and Dirk had a mop of thick, dark hair, neatly combed back, and fun-loving eyes behind his formal-looking steel-rimmed round glasses. They had been married eight years and did not have any children.

I called my 'foster parents' Uncle Dirk and Aunt Ella. To protect myself, and them, my name was changed to 'Verdoren' and if anyone asked, I had a false background story about my mother; telling people that the only reason I wasn't at home with her was because she was 'in a hospital in Switzerland' and couldn't come back because of the war. I now find that totally unbelievable, but no-one questioned it at the time.

It was actually Uncle Dirk's brother, Cornelis Rijnders (also in the resistance), who found this home for me. To me he was 'Uncle Henk,' which was his alias. He was very brave and looked after lots of Jewish people in lots of ways – such as giving out false ration cards and identity cards. And yet he found the time to arrange to have my own bicycle sent to me in Woubrugge, and to write me a note saying he hoped I was doing well and that my bicycle would soon be there. Uncle Henk did not survive the war. He was arrested and shot on 25 April 1944 by members of a notorious group of Dutch Nazi police officers, in the north of the Netherlands. His body was found the next day in a canal next to where he had been shot.

Yoka told me she was made as welcome at the local school as she was at Jacobswoude. It was a public school for Protestant children and she loved singing hymns and psalms, and hearing stories from the bible. She also recalled 'fitting in perfectly with the other children, not least because I had blue eyes and blond pigtails'.

She said that because of this school she developed a Christian faith and that after the war the Bible stories she had learnt proved invaluable in her later studies, even though she eventually shed her Christian beliefs. She also said that after the war her father, a lifelong atheist, tried to explain that there was no God. She said, 'I silently decided not to argue with him since I knew I could not win the argument, but in my 10-year-old mind I knew I was right.'

Yoka also made a lifelong friend with the girl who lived next door; her name was Miny van Wijk. Her father owned a shipyard, and the two of them spent many happy hours playing in the yard and together at each other's homes. She mentioned, too, that:

Miny and I remained friends and visited each other until Miny's death in 2016, when we were both over 80. Her brother Bouwe was a classmate of mine. I was very much a part of the Woubrugge community, playing marbles and jump rope in the school yard and jumping across the wide ditches between meadows in the summer. In winter we skated on the canal next to our homes.

Dirk and Ella Rijnders' kindness towards people who needed to be hidden did not, however, stop with Yoka. Far from it; their home became a busy refuge for many others and was also a local meeting point for members of the resistance to gather together. She said:

I did not know at the time that the convivial evening 'smoker's meetings' held regularly at the house were actually meetings of the local underground. Two weeks before the end of the war, Uncle Dirk was asked to provide names and addresses of men suitable for labour in Germany. At that point, cooperation was no longer an option for him, and the Rijnders family went into hiding themselves, with the mayor of the next village.

One of the other people who hid at the Rijnders home, was Mr Santberg, who was a pale young man who belonged to the Dutch aristocracy. He was employed by Uncle Dirk at the town hall so that he could avoid forced labour in Germany. Unfortunately, he decided at one point that he absolutely had to visit his aged parents; he was shot and killed near his family home while trying to avoid arrest.

And towards the end of the war, during the Hongerwinter of 1944–45, starving people from the cities who needed extra nourishment in order to survive lived with us for a few weeks. The local farmers saw to it that we had enough to eat. All the same, I remember sugar beets were boiled for long periods on the potbellied stove in hopes of producing sugar. We also ate tulip bulbs a few times. They were tasteless.

Yoka also told me that at one point a German soldier lived with them. This was because the Germans, still occupying the country, ordered local homeowners to accommodate their troops. A very memorable moment occurred for Yoka when she found out exactly who the latest inhabitant was. She said:

The soldier was put up in what had been our dining room, next to the kitchen. He was probably an ordinary young fellow, also far from home. When Aunt Ella introduced me, he wanted to shake my hand to which I reacted by promptly putting my hand behind my back. Aunt Ella told me years later that this was one of the most frightening moments of the war for her.

Yoka mentioned, too, a couple of other poignant and special moments of this time that have stayed with her. One was during a visit to Ella's parents in November 1943; she said that whilst she was staying with them (happily too; they were as kind as their daughter) she received a note telling her Dirk and Ella had had a baby and had named her 'Roosje'. Yoka says she and Roosje were lifelong 'sisters' until she died in 2002.

Finally, days before liberation, when the Rijnders themselves had to go into hiding, Yoka had to go elsewhere too. She was taken in by the school principal Mr Mooijaart and his wife. She said that the day after the Netherlands was liberated, Mr Mooijaart addressed the class and told them: 'Today Yoka Verdoren is Yoka Verdoner again' – words that have moved her deeply ever since.

Yoka also recalled sleeping in a small attic room on the third floor, just under the roof. She said:

When I stood on a chair, I could look out of the small dormer windows over the meadows stretching out into the far distance. On spring and summer evenings, when I was assumed to be sound asleep, I often stood there and looked out for a long time at the flowering trees and beautiful peaceful meadows.

I also remember my fear during the last year of the war when Allied planes shot at any transport on the roads and the canals. One morning, some ships that had anchored right next to our house were attacked. I was deathly afraid and screamed at the top of my lungs. After that, I spent many nights shaking in my bed, as I imagined hearing ships and aircraft approaching our house at the same time and thinking I was even closer to those aircraft in that attic room than on the ground.

Finally, in May 1945, liberation! One day soon afterwards, I saw a familiar figure walking up the long driveway to the house. It was my 24-year-old cousin Albert, who had spent the war years in hiding in Amsterdam and who had now come to look for me. Although I had totally forgotten his existence, I recognised him immediately. He was family — in a different and more profound sense than those who had loved and protected me during the war years. I knew then the war was completely over.

It was, indeed, over. Germany was no longer in control and the Dutch people were free to re-build their shattered lives. For some weeks Yoka continued to live with the Rijnders, during which time Uncle Dick took her to Amsterdam where she was reunited with her father. Of this reunion, for which she was naturally very excited about, she said:

I am sure we hugged and kissed when we saw each other and that he then told me where my little brother and younger sister were and his hopes to be able to reunite us as soon as possible. But what I remember with absolute clarity is one piece of the conversation. 'Do you think Mama is coming back?

I must have known by then that she had been arrested and sent somewhere or killed, although nothing was known yet for certain. My father, who believed in being straightforward, said, 'I don't think so.' And I do remember my response, 'You never think something like that is going to happen to *you*.'

However, whilst the war was over, for children like Yoka – European Jewish children who lost so much due to the trauma, turmoil and tragic loss – it was never completely over because the scars inflicted by their emotional suffering did not ever truly heal. Yoka has spoken publicly about her own feelings in this regard, as well as about her brother and sister – suggesting that perhaps their suffering has been even more acute because they were younger, therefore totally unable to have any comprehension at all of why their lives were turned so completely upside down.

Writing in the *Guardian*, in June 2018[5] these are Yoka's words about her brother Otto and sister Francisca:

> Have you heard the screams and seen the panic of a three-year-old when it has lost sight of its mother in a supermarket? That scream subsides when mother reappears around the end of the aisle.

This is my brother writing in recent years. He tries to deal with his lasting pain through memoir. It's been 76 years, yet he revisits the separation obsessively. He still writes about it in the present tense:

> In the first home I scream for six weeks. Then I am moved to another family, and I stop screaming. I give up. Nothing around me is known to me. All those around me are strangers. I have no past. I have no future. I have no identity. I am nowhere. I am frozen in fear. It is the only emotion I possess now. As a three-year-old child, I believe that I must have made some terrible mistake to have caused my known world to disappear. I spend the rest of my life trying desperately not to make another mistake.

My brother's second foster family cared deeply about him and has kept in touch with him all these years. Even so, he is almost 80 years old now and is still trying to understand what made him the anxious and dysfunctional person he turned into as a child and has remained for the rest of his life: a man with charm and intelligence, yet who could never keep a job because of his inability to complete tasks. After all, if he persisted, he might make a mistake again, and that would bring his world to another end.

My younger sister was separated from our parents at five. She had no understanding of what was going on and why she suddenly had to live with a strange set of adults. She suffered thereafter from lifelong, profound depression.

Yoka's father took the three of them to America in November 1946, where they settled in New York City as best they could, but it was a difficult time for them. His war had also been immensely unsettling: hiding in different places, missing his children and of course suffering the loss of his wife. Yoka told me that his parents were killed on the same day as his wife. After the war the family found themselves in financial difficulties, too, because his business partner had stolen most of the money in their firm; worse still, his partner betrayed him further by telling the government Yoka's father had conducted business with Germans, and he was briefly sent to prison. He was not well, either; he suffered with ulcers, and in the spring of 1947 he fell ill with cancer and died in October that year. The three children lived with their father's sister and husband after his death, but this was not an easy time for them either, such was their grief and feelings of displacement. Francisca eventually married and had three children, and Otto became a father of two; but all three bore the scars of war for their whole lives.

Yoka has spent most of her life in California, working as a teacher and a psychotherapist, but she has returned to the Netherlands many times, and also lived in Israel for a while. She believes that because of what happened to her she learnt to be very independent from a young age and take care of herself. She told me she never married or had a lasting relationship – her inability to commit, or need anyone, being a consequence of her difficult childhood. She said: 'I have lived with a feeling that often I don't belong'; it is a feeling that has followed her wherever she has been.

But her warm feelings toward her wartime home remain:

Even years after the war, when I returned as an adult, the farmers would greet me. They all still knew me as 'Yoka van de burgemeester', - the mayor's Yoka.

I have chosen to end Yoka's story by copying the words of a letter sent by her mother, Hilde Verdoner-Sluizer, to her father, Gerrit, while she was being held in Westerbork, the Nazi transit camp in the Netherlands. While he had been able to avoid capture and was in hiding, she had been arrested and was in captivity in Westerbork for about fifteen months, from November 1942 until February 1944 — the month she was 'called up for transport' to Auschwitz, where she was killed. In their book *Signs of Life*[6] Yoka and her sister Francisca published the letters Hilde wrote to her husband, which were somehow smuggled out of the camp. The letters tell of conditions in the camp and how she coped during this traumatic time. The letters also reveal why she did not escape when she had the opportunity because she feared her parents, brother and parents-in-law would suffer immediate deportation to the death camps in reprisal. As time passed Hilde realised that she, too, would not leave alive but would succumb to the same fate as many of those she saw disappear.

Yoka has given me permission to quote from one of the letters; I have chosen one sent by Hilde in January 1943. Hilde writes of survival and strength, even saying at the end, 'everything has its advantages and disadvantages, here as everywhere.' Yoka, her daughter, is of course the protagonist for this chapter, our Remarkable Woman – but certainly, her mother was remarkable too.

Yoka Verdoner, *c.* 2008.

Dear Gerrit

...

On re-reading this letter [*referring to the part of the letter she had just written*], I thought it turned out to be such a lousy one, all in all, that I would prefer not to send it. However, since I did not want to leave you without news any longer, and since it may be a long time before I can write you a better letter, you'll have to take it as it is. I do hope you are well, and that you will have the good sense to go on as best you can, even though it may be very difficult for you. That, after all, is the only way we have a chance of surviving. Take good care of your health and stay calm. Spend as much time as possible with friends, either in the van Breestraat or at Fen and Jan's. Also around the Pretoriusstraat where we have so many good friends.

Don't dwell on how beautiful and pleasant life could have been, because one always tends to idealize things and we have to get through this anyway. Also, please don't think that I do not sympathize with your problems, but on the larger scale of things they are so insignificant, and you really have to have the conviction that the strength to survive all this has to come from within and that no-one, not even the most ideal spouse or anyone else, can help you if you do not muster all your own strength.

I shall try to write to you again soon and, if possible, tell you a bit more about my daily activities here. I am doing well, and most importantly, I am healthy and always busy at work. Last week's cold spell had the great advantage that we had *no* mud for a couple of days. After the thaw, the mud was virtually impossible to trudge through. As you can see, everything has its advantages and disadvantages, here as everywhere.

Lots of love and kisses from,

Hilde

NOTES

1 *Holocaust Encyclopedia* (ushmm.org), United States Holocaust Memorial Museum
2 encyclopedia.ushmm.org/content/en/article/plight-of-jewish-children
3 holland.com/global/tourism/holland-stories/liberation-route/hollands-occupation-during-wwii
4 Ingrid de Zwarte, *De Hongerwinter*, Prometheus, 2019
5 Yoka Verdoner, 'The Nazis separated me from my parents as a child. The trauma lasts a lifetime', *The Guardian*, June 2018
6 Yoka Verdoner and Francisca Verdoner-Kan eds, *Signs of Life: The Letters of Hilde Verdoner-Sluizer*, Acropolis Books Ltd, 1990

MIDORI YAMAZAKI: THE MEMORY OF A JAPANESE TEENAGER

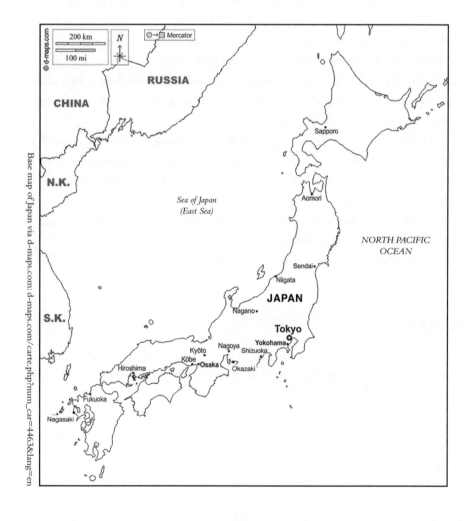

Base map of Japan via d-maps.com: d-maps.com/carte.php?num_car=4463&lang=en

Affectionately known as 'Chibi' (which means 'little one' in Japanese), Midori Yamazaki was the smallest, and youngest, of around 200 people employed at a parachute factory in the Japanese town of Okazaki during the war, all working long hours, knowing that what they were creating was an essential item for every airman forced to take to the sky. Without such a safety net there was no hope for any of the airmen – at all – should they be shot down in the course of duty.

Midori was just 14 years old when she began working here in the spring of 1944. She had not wanted to take up this position at all, but she knew it was important, necessary work – hundreds of factories throughout Japan were intensifying their production of all sorts of items needed as the war continued: weapons, explosives, artillery and sundry items, including protective clothes and medical kits, all needed to be manufactured as quickly as possible. Many factories were struggling to find enough people to work in them, particularly because so many men had gone off to fight; Midori was one of thousands to step into the breach. And what a huge step it was; Okazaki (located towards the south of central Japan, in between Kyoto to the west and Tokyo to the east) was over 170km from her northern hometown of Nanbu-cho, and there was no easy way to travel there – in those days it was a slow train journey, with lots of changes, taking around eighteen hours.

However, deciding the pay would be useful too, Midori and a friend of hers decided to take up the challenge of employment, doing their 'bit' for their country after their town was visited by officials from the parachute manufacturer, and other factories, looking for people to fill empty positions. Midori's six years of compulsory schooling had finished a year before; she was bright and would have liked to continue in education, but her parents didn't have enough money anyway – so she made the brave decision to do what she felt was the 'right' thing.

Not surprisingly, Midori and her friend were both very homesick after arriving in Okazaki, especially during the first few months. She had left not only her mother and father but her big, close family; she was one of eight siblings – the second eldest, with four sisters and three brothers. Okazaki, too, was very different to Nanbu-cho – it was a large, industrial town whereas her hometown was a small farming village. Her father, a carpenter, was exempt from going to the front line when the war in the Far East began in 1941 because he was too old, and her eldest brother, the only member of the family of the right age to be called up, also escaped going to the front line because at the time he was needed he had appendicitis. Midori knew all her family (with the exception of her eldest brother, who was working in an electrical factory in Yokahama, some 80 miles away) were back at home and she missed them very much.

Midori and her friend were accommodated at the parachute factory; they slept on futon mattresses in a dormitory, which they shared with other women who had started working there at roughly the same time as they did. It was hard graft, during a time of immense worry and exhaustion, as the war was showing no signs of abating. The two young girls were not actually allowed to go home during the first year, but after a few months they bravely made the decision to escape during the night and made it all the way back to Nanbu-cho. It was, indeed, a daring escapade – involving an initial risky dash through the factory, avoiding security, walking in the dark to the local train station, finally making it back to their hometown at midnight, after catching the first of many trains at Okazaki at 6 a.m. However, after a few days at home the two young girls were persuaded that they should return to the factory; so their long journey began again, this time in reverse ...

I would like to think it was not, perhaps, quite so hard after their return. Their successful return home, and just seeing their family albeit for a short time, must have been strengthening and uplifting for them – even though reprimands were almost certainly involved. And there was someone quite special waiting for Midori to return to the factory – 'Sha'. Sha was the Chinese cook at the factory who, after all these years, she remembers with fondness because he was so kind, probably to all, but possibly especially to Midori. It was Sha who nicknamed Midori 'Chibi'; and, she said, he gave her extra food too, in secret, when others weren't looking. Sha, she said, would proudly show her letters from his daughter, who was about the same age as 'Chibi' – which she was delighted to look at, even though she couldn't read them because they were in Chinese. Midori said Sha cooked them the most delicious food he could, even though it wasn't always easy to make it very tasty given the limited ingredients available. His 'best' food, she recalled, were his steamed buns – she said everyone always looked forward to 'Sha's buns'.

Midori's work at the factory ended in the summer of 1945; by this time parachute production there had almost ceased because there was a shortage of material – indeed there was a shortage of material for many vital things (even the Japanese air force were resorting to using pine resin as fuel because they didn't have enough petrol) – and instead of making parachutes she was making soap out of silkworm cocoons. There was plenty of work for her, indeed for many, but by June 1945 the Second World War in the West had concluded with victory to the Allies, and Japan was rapidly becoming a very dangerous place indeed – with the Allies (led by the Americans in this part of the world) determined to conclude the war here, too, as soon as possible. The intense, strategic bombing campaign, which ended with the dropping of the atomic bombs over Nagasaki and Hiroshima at the beginning of August 1945, had intensified. Midori's mother was terrified for her 'Chibi' and wanted her home. She sent a telegram to the factory falsely declaring that Midori's father was 'dangerously ill', requesting her speedy return. The factory owners were duly sympathetic, bringing an end to her work in the factory.

Midori acknowledged that whilst her mother's action in sending an untrue telegram was almost certainly 'non-patriotic', it did very likely save her life. On 20 June 1945, just days after Midori's departure, Okazaki was struck by over 12,000 incendiary bombs that led to the immediate deaths of over 200 people and destroyed a third of the city. The bombs directly targeted civilians – including strafing people queuing up at a medical centre. The attack was part of the strategic bombing campaign waged by America against military and civilian targets in Japan during the closing months of the Second World War in the Pacific.[1]

I doubt, from the way Midori described how circumstances were unfold-ing, questioning the ethics of whether to declare a falsehood to potentially save her daughter's life really came into her mother's decision-making. Her brother in Yokohama had narrowly escaped being killed during a bombing raid over the city on 29 May; the factory he was working in was targeted, together with many other buildings. Whilst he escaped, 8,000 others did not and lost their lives. Midori said it was nearly losing her brother that prompted her mother's telegram to her factory. Midori, too, before she left Okazaki, was more than aware of the risks because of the regular attacks that were inflicted on the city of Nagoya, which was only around 30km from Okazaki. Nagoya was a prime target for the Americans because it was the centre of the Japanese aircraft industry; it was in factories here that around half of Japan's combat aircraft and engines were manufactured. No other city, apart from Tokyo, was struck more than Nagoya. Midori recalled how terrifying it was for her during these raids, even though they were 30km away. She said that during these raids they would hide in shelters that would shake 'as if there was an earthquake', and because the Americans used incendiary bombs, whilst the city 'burnt', the sky was continually 'bright with fire'.

All of these raids (Tokyo, Nagoya, Okazaki, Yokohama) – and many others besides – were so-called 'strategic' because they were part of a clear and determined campaign by the Americans to bring the war in the Pacific to an end with the implementation of this strategy, which was to destroy Japan's ability to continue to develop and maintain its own warfare infrastructure, and to attack civilians in order to damage morale. The attack on Okazaki was by no means the most awful in terms of lives lost; but that fact does not lessen the pain caused to those who suffered – in whatever respect – because of it. Whilst even larger-scale attacks (such as those over Hiroshima and Nagasaki in August 1945 that brought this campaign – indeed the whole war – to an end) invariably create more headlines and are better-known, behind every individual that is killed there is (usually) a family who grieves, and the suffering of any human being – wherever they are, whoever they are and whatever that suffering is – is painful, emotionally and/or physically. It is important we remember all those who suffered during this strategic campaign, including the lesser-known attacks on places like Okazaki, as well as those who suffered so very much, during the attacks we know far more about.

★★★

Midori Yamazaki (born Watanabe) is now 91 years old, and lives in Fuji city in Shizuoka with her husband Ichiro, who is 88. She kindly recalled her memories of the Second World War for me through her daughter, Harumi, whom I was introduced to by Fiona Symon, whose contribution to this book is about the sinking of the *Lancastria* in the summer of 1940. Fiona and Harumi live not far from each other in Scotland and are firm friends, united in part in their care for, and interest in, Second World War history. Fiona proudly spoke to me of her friendship with Harumi, also making it clear to me that there is no awkwardness between them because they were on 'different sides' during the war. I am touched and glad that Fiona trusted me enough to introduce me to Harumi, not only so that I am able to include a chapter about the Second World War in the Far East, but also because she knows my writing is not political; the purpose of my writing is to convey real accounts of what it was like for those who lived through it. As I want this book to include as wide a variety of Second World War memories as possible, a Japanese chapter is not only appropriate, but also necessary.

I am touched that Harumi understands this, so much so that she approached her mother and arranged it so I could include this chapter. She told me that when she told her parents of her engagement to a British man, Ian (Currie), her mother's response was, 'What will you do if Britain and Japan start a war again?'; to which Harumi told her she would do all she could to ensure such a conflict would 'never happen again'. As good as her word, since marrying Ian in 1989, in addition to her work in translation and as a Japanese teacher, she has worked to promote peace and support the rights of women, regardless of religion, as a member of the Women's Federation for World Peace, for which she was chairperson of the Scottish chapter.

★★★

The Empire of Japan officially entered the Second World War over a year after it began in Europe, on 27 September 1940, with the signing of the Tripartite Pact with Germany and Italy. However, it wasn't until December 1941 that Japan entered the war in earnest, with the bombing of Pearl Harbor in Hawaii, which was the central hub of the whole of the American navy. Whilst the attack was not completely unexpected, its scale, ferocity and success took the Americans by surprise – and they were furious. This led to the Americans joining the war effort for the Allies, and the war in the Far East truly began.

Shortly after Pearl Harbor and throughout 1942, Japan launched military offensives on many islands and against Allied forces in the East including Hong Kong, Burma, Malaya, Thailand and the Dutch East Indes, with many of the battles also taking place in the surrounding Pacific and Indian Oceans. The war in the Far East is most generally known as the Pacific War because this is, very much, an island area. It was also, geographically, the largest theatre of war in the world. Many of the key battles took place 'at sea', where the US Navy Pacific Fleet deployed a vast range of aircraft carriers, destroyers and submarines. To give an idea of the enormity of the battles, June 1944 was the scene of the largest aircraft-carrier battle in history, taking place in the Philippine Sea, involving 15 American fleet and light carriers, 9 Japanese carriers, 170 other warships, and some 1,700 other aircraft.[2] The battle itself lasted just two days, but it resulted in the deaths of nearly 3,000 members of the Japanese navy and the loss of around 650 of their aircraft.

However, Japanese civilian families such as Midori's were relatively unscathed by the activity going on in the islands, and in the ocean that surrounded them. The most painful impact of war that would have been felt by them was if a family member had had to go to fight, causing them turmoil and anxiety – a feeling shared the world over by family members left behind because of the war. That said, the Japanese on the mainland were hit economically during these first couple of years – vast amounts of money were being spent on armoury, defensive materiel and war machinery. Workers in factories (including Midori) had to work hard to 'churn out' what was needed; and of course, inevitably, a general feeling of fear hung over the Japanese people.

The way the Second World War in the East was being played out then changed completely in the summer of 1944, with the launch of the American strategic bombing campaign – which was when the attacks on the mainland began – and the Japanese people, including families like Midori's, could not escape it. Almost half a million Japanese civilians died during this campaign, which continued for over a year and during which tens of thousands of incendiary bombs were dropped on sixty-six cities in Japan.

With no Japanese surrender occurring, the Americans eventually succeeded in bringing the Pacific War to an end with the dropping of two atomic bombs: over Hiroshima and Nagasaki in August 1945 – killing around 120,000 and 80,000 almost immediately. Almost as many died of the consequential radiation leaks within the following weeks.

The Emperor of Japan at the time, Emperor Hirohito, eventually surrendered on 15 August, and a period of Allied occupation, with political and economic assistance, continued well into the 1950s.

★★★

It was a defeat that left behind a most awful mess of a country, brought about in the most brutal circumstances imaginable, and resulting in a society scarred, bruised, damaged and crushed in almost every conceivable way.

Midori spoke about how very difficult everything was after the war. She spoke about how hungry people were because food was rationed but the rations did not provide enough for people to live on. She recalled how they had to simply eat whatever they could get – remembering 'runners' of sweet potato, which were horrible but at least kept starvation at bay. Because they lived in the countryside, she and her family were the 'lucky ones'. The situation, she said, was far worse in the cities. She recalled, too, how people from the city would travel to their village just to exchange some of their clothes for a bag of rice.

She spoke, too, of 'black markets' everywhere, and markets selling such things as old second-hand shoes and second-hand clothes that the Americans didn't want any more, in addition to black-market alcohol – much of which was highly dangerous industrial methyl alcohol. Many who consumed it went blind, including one of Midori's uncles.

Midori did return to Okazaki after the war to work again, but she didn't go to the same factory. She said that when she disembarked the train at Okazaki, she wasn't sure 'where she was' because it was barely recognisable.

Midori worked for some of the post-war years in Okazaki, and back at home in Nanbu-cho, making kimonos and working as a maid and nanny. In 1956 she married Ichiro Yamazaki and in 1957 Harumi, their eldest of two children, was born. Together, they set up a flower shop in Takaoka, in Fuji city. The shop continues to this day, bringing joy and colour into people's homes and offices and into their lives.

Midori Yamazaki, *c.* 2018.

Japan is renowned for much that is unique, beautiful and fascinating, including its tea ceremonies, sushi, calligraphy and flower-arranging. However, when I think of Japan (I have had the joy of travelling there, in the spring of 2001), I think of the blossom. Every year, in April, Japan's *sakura* (cherry blossoms) brighten up roads, parks and avenues; it is hard not to feel joyful just thinking of the gentle pink canopy that almost warms the air with its colour then drops, slowly, silently to the ground creating a sumptuous carpet of pink softness. From there the blossom petals slowly disappear into the earth, until blossoming again, year after year. It is strange and sobering to think that when the bombs fell in Japan in April 1945, so too did the blossom; I expect the *sakura* was hardly noticed. But as the years pass since the falling of those bombs, such symbols of peace, I think, become ever more important.

NOTES

1 John Vader, 'Marianas Islands and Japan, December 1944/May 1945' in *Purnell's History of the Second World War*, Vol. 6, Phoebus Publishing Ltd, c. 1970
2 www.britannica.com/event/Battle-of-the-Philippine-Sea

MOLLIE BIRCH: A MOTHER'S STORY OF TRAVELLING FROM BURMA TO INDIA

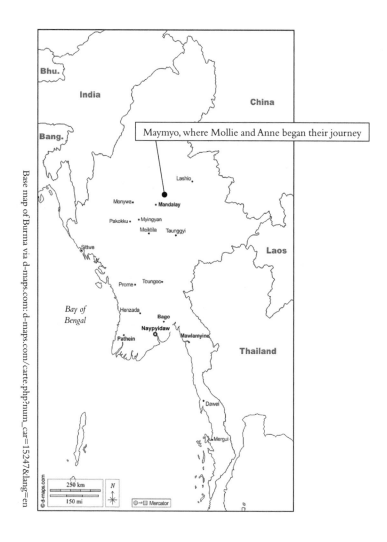

Maymyo, where Mollie and Anne began their journey

Base map of Burma via d-maps.com: d-maps.com/carte.php?num_car=15247&lang=en

Bhu.

India

China

Bang.

Lashio

Monywa • Mandalay

Pakokku • Myingyan

Maiktila Taunggyi

Sittwe

Laos

Prome Tcungoo

Bay of
Bengal

Henzada

Bago

Naypyidaw

Pathein

Mawlamyine

Thailand

Dawei

Mergui

250 km

150 mi

N

⊙→☐ Mercator

Whilst each chapter in this book, and those in its companion book *Remarkable Journeys of the Second World War*,[1] reveals an individual memory of the war, at the same time the memory described also tells the story of thousands more who could not – or did not – tell their story. Often when I am writing up a memory I think about those other people and how they might have coped in that situation – those younger, older, weaker, more frightened perhaps, hungrier or possibly more despairing.

I am mentioning this in a brief introduction to Mollie Birch's chapter because her memory tells of her journey out of Burma to India, after the Japanese began their invasion in 1941; and those of you who have read *Remarkable Journeys* will know that that book contains a memory of the same journey, albeit written up in a very different way. I urge those of you who find Mollie's chapter compelling to read Pat Rorke's story in *Remarkable Journeys*. Both stories are heart-warming accounts of determined women caring for others as they travelled, whilst being exhausted themselves, and equally saddened by leaving Burma – a country they both loved – and both knowing nothing of what awaited them.

I learnt so much about Burma when I was writing Pat's chapter. She spoke to me not only about the impact of the war and her journey, but about the birds, trees, food and people; I was so pleased when I came across Mollie's story and thus had an opportunity to 'return' to the delightful Burmese colours, smells and sounds Pat introduced me to because (of course in common with all the stories) there is so much more to write!

Mollie Birch was a young mother given no choice but to undertake this exhausting trek with her young daughter, whereas Pat Rorke – whose story is in my earlier book – was in her late teens, so she did not have the responsibility Mollie had; but both of course were journeying to a destination unknown, both fearful and apprehensive. There are further similarities – both women travelled northwards out of Burma, through Bangladesh, to the safety of India. Both women loved Burma and were very sorry to have to leave. But that is where the similarities end; their different experiences as they travelled reveal just how much could still be written about the war – Mollie and Pat are but two of thousands who undertook this journey alone. Both stories are fascinating and important in their own ways.

I would like to think Mollie and Pat might have met en route, but I shall never know; that lovely thought must stay in my imagination.

★★★

It was not until September 1941 that Mollie Birch began to appreciate there really was a war unfolding in the world around her. At that time, she was living in Burma with her husband Fred and daughter Ann, who was 2½ years old. They lived in the garrison town of Maymyo in the north of the country – a small, pretty town, with lovely gardens, overlooked by hills and lakes. Their home was a compact, modern bungalow; they were one of around sixty couples and families living in the cantonment, enjoying the climate, the food and each other's company. Maymyo's shopping area was small, but they lacked nothing; fruit, vegetables and flowers were plentiful and the town's one and only shop had everything else they needed.

Fred was serving in Burma as an orderly officer for the Kings Own Yorkshire Light Infantry (KOYLI) – a regiment of the British Army. As the orderly officer he oversaw the security and administration of the unit, and was often on guard at night as well as during the day, ensuring the troops were attentive, properly dressed and generally conducting themselves in an appropriate manner.

Fred, in common with all the troops, had to be prepared for the reality of war; but of course, no one had any idea when (or if) the bitter pain of the conflict would suddenly be upon them. 'At the ready', the KOYLIs all had a small kitbag packed with jungle kit, tin hat, identity disc, mug and plate – and none were ever far from their rifle. The men would leave their wives sometimes during these early, 'pain-free' months of the Second World War for a night, or sometimes two, but rarely longer. These departures were training exercises and/or visits to the not-so-faraway Burmese jungle that they knew one day might be their battleground.

During the night in September 1941 Fred left for guard duty: nothing unusual in that. Mollie had boiled the kettle and prepared a pot of tea, as she always did, in anticipation of his return at the expected time. But on this occasion when he returned, he barely had time to drink his tea. That night, in the early hours, all he did was pick up his kitbag and leave. Shortly afterwards, Mollie recalled the sounding of a 'bugle', which she knew meant the men were off for another trip to the jungle. She expected then she would see him in one or maybe a couple of days. But on this occasion, he did not return so soon. Mollie Birch did not see her husband again until July 1942.

★★★

This chapter is Mollie Birch's Second World War story; it tells of her traumatic journey out of Burma to the safety of India, accompanied by one other wife, Mary Birdsall, and her three children Raymond, Joyce and Lorna – also without husband and father, also fearing not only the present but a future unknown. Mollie died in 2002. Her – true – testimony is contained in a letter she wrote to her daughter Ann, who has given it to me so that I can tell her mother's story; in doing so, I am telling the story of the other, equally courageous and equally frightened, woman and children who travelled with her.

However, before I write of Mollie's journey, with extracts from her letter, I will set out what was happening in Burma at the time; how and why the harsh reality of the Second World War forced her departure, with Ann, to India.

★★★

Burma is one of the largest countries in Asia, sitting between Thailand to the south-east and Bangladesh to the north-west; directly in the west, on the other side of the Bay of Bengal, is India. Burma is now known as 'Myanmar', following a name change in 1989, and its largest city Rangoon changed its name at the same time to 'Yangon'. However, as I re-tell Mollie's story, I will use the old names of Burma and Rangoon, as this is what they were during the Second World War.

As I have mentioned at the start of this chapter, Burma was moderately peaceful until the latter part of 1941. In September that year Fred departed for the jungle, along with most of the men of his regiment, leaving the wives and children behind in Maymyo. The weeks that followed, until December, remained calm; but, of course, for those left behind, the worry and uncertainty was immense.

However, the situation in Burma began to alter dramatically for everyone after the Japanese bombed the American naval station of Pearl Harbor, in Hawaii, on 7 December 1941. The attack, not least of all because of its scale and ferocity – 360 Japanese warplanes dropping bombs and incendiaries that killed nearly 2,500 US servicemen (and some civilians) and injuring many more – took the Americans by surprise.[2]

Up until that point the two countries had been attempting to keep rather fragile diplomatic relations, over such things as trade, continuing. Both were important industrial powers aware of their interdependency, which had been developing since the beginning of the century. America had established colonies in Asia and the Pacific to secure natural resources for themselves and a market for their goods; Japan was one of their main customers for such things as steel and petrol. However, in the 1930s relations began to falter as the two nations developed opposing ideas, particularly about the economic and political future of China. Japan invaded its neighbour in 1931 and needed the supplies from America to keep its battle with China going. America continued to supply Japan with what it needed, both for China and in Japan, including domestic fuel, but by 1941 Japan – in alliance with Germany – was invading other nations, including French Indochina. America, under President Roosevelt, decided that 'enough was enough', and in the summer of that year it cut off oil supplies to Japan entirely. That decision, by the Americans, was almost certainly a pre-cursor to the attack.

However, President Roosevelt was furious, as well as surprised, by what happened on 7 December. The Japanese had wreaked havoc on the US Navy, undoubtedly preparing itself for full-scale war in the Pacific, in which Burma would be intrinsically involved. That day the US Navy lost five out of eight battleships, three destroyers and 200 aircraft – as well as a huge number of personnel. Fortunately, three of its aircraft carriers happened to be out at sea on a training exercise. The Japanese attack was strategically and meticulously planned and executed. It is said that part of the reason for the American's surprise was that it had not occurred to them that the Japanese were capable of doing what they did.

President Roosevelt's actions following the bombing were swift and decisive. Speaking to Congress the day after the bombing, he famously said, 'Yesterday, December 7, 1941–a date which will live in infamy–the United States of America was suddenly and deliberately attacked by naval and air forces of the Empire of Japan.' Following this speech, upon his request to Congress, a resolution recognising a state of war between the US and Japan was approved. Three days later Germany declared war against America.

Thus, the scene was set for a huge change in the whole theatre of the Second World War. America had put itself at the heart of the conflict. The American contribution to the successful war effort spanned four years, resulting in the deaths of some 400,000 Americans, including a number who died in the campaign in Burma.

The Japanese began their invasion into Burma in January 1942, initially aiming to cut off the Burma Road because this was the route by which China was now being supplied with vital armoury by the Americans and the British, which China needed in order to defend itself in its long-running dispute with Japan. However, possibly even more important was the Japanese plan to occupy Burma; indeed – in partnership with Germany – to occupy by using whatever means necessary, wherever it could, in order to reign supreme.

★★★

'We knew,' wrote Mollie:

> That after the Japanese attacked America there was trouble ahead, and war would cease to be a word, but a reality. After that, all over Maymyo air-raid trenches were dug and sirens screamed.
>
> Ann, you and I were allocated places in a trench not too far from our bungalow. When the siren went, we had to get to the trench as quickly as possible. You were two and half so we made a game of it because I knew it would be quicker for you to run on your own and me to follow, than to carry you. If our Ayah or Bearer were near, they would take you to the trench. If not, as soon as the siren sounded, you would be away. By the time I arrived you were so excited and always greeted me with 'Mummy, I was first!'

I should just take a moment to mention here that the journey which will shortly be described was even more of a challenge for Mollie than it was for most because she suffered with a condition that affected her mobility. Her legs were different lengths – the left one being 4in shorter than the right because one of her hips had been dislocated at birth. Mollie, therefore, had a twisted spine, difficulty balancing and needed to wear a built-up shoe on her left foot.

Whilst in Maymyo Mollie and Ann received a lot of help and care from their 'Ayah' (house servant) because they were British, living in a British colony. Ann thinks, in part because of the support she received, her mother's

Mollie Birch with her
daughter Ann, *c.*1941.

time in Maymyo before the bombing was probably the happiest time of her
life. Departing, therefore, as they had to, and in the way that they did, was
exceptionally hard for both mother and daughter.

★★★

Before Mollie and Ann's journey began, in January 1942, the then small
population of Maymyo began to expand quite dramatically as they were
joined by British families who had been stationed near Rangoon, but for
whom remaining there was far too dangerous. Accommodation – everything
– had to be shared, and Mollie and Ann took in a lady called Mrs O'Neill
who had a 3-year-old daughter, Jill. Mollie wrote, 'We agreed very well for
the few weeks we were together,' but these were frightening, uncertain times:

> Blackout was introduced because now the siren really did mean an air-raid.
> Several times, day after day, the Japanese planes flew over. They dropped bombs

only once, so little damage was done but it caused havoc for the Burmese and Indians who disappeared into the jungle for days. Shops were left open and there was a lot of looting. I had a 'gem' of a bearer. If he heard of an 'open' shop he would cycle off and get what he thought we needed. Bread was the most difficult thing to get. I remember being in the town once, near the bakers, after an 'all clear.' I went back to the shop – the baker and his staff had gone, and people were just helping themselves to bread and cakes. I did so want a loaf, at home all we had were a few stale slices. I was so tempted to just help myself; it was the nearest I have ever become of being a thief! But I waited, hoping the baker would return so I could buy from him, but the bread disappeared before he returned, so I was left with nothing – but when I got home my bearer, Anthony, was there with two loaves. No doubt he had stolen them, but I paid for them anyway …

The Japanese had a habit of raiding us at mealtimes, so we started having breakfast and lunch at about 10.30 and calling it brunch.

It was during a 'brunch', in early February 1942, that Mollie Birch's evacuation journey began. She, with Ann and another British family from Maymyo, suddenly received an order to pack their bags and be ready to depart by 2 p.m. the same day. She was told the maximum weight of belongings for herself and Ann was 44lb, including food for four days, mosquito net, pillow, blanket and strong walking shoes. The departure order, she wrote, came as a shock:

It is difficult to express my feelings of that time. We had a very nice home and had bought all our furniture because in those days army furniture was dreadful. This was also our first home together and we really did take pride in it. Just pause for a moment, look around your home and imagine how you would feel leaving so much. Believe me, the smallest thing becomes a treasure. A week before we had had this notice several of the families had left to hike to India. We thought we were on a hike. I had visions, Ann, of you and I gradually falling behind the British party, then getting further and further away, the Japanese getting nearer and you and I in between. However, I did not have time to worry about that. I had to get packing.

At 1.30 pm I had another notice telling me not to leave at 2 pm but to await further instructions. It had been decided that, owing to my affliction, we would be flown out of Burma with the expectant mums. Mrs O'Neill and Jill went off in army lorries at about 2 o'clock. Anthony and my Ayah asked if they could go too. I was sorry to say goodbye.

After they left, I felt very alone; most of the houses were empty. The place seemed dead. I dared not leave the house to see who else had left in case someone else was coming with another notice. I waited and waited, had tea and then at around 8 pm I put you to bed, still dressed. Still, I waited, listening to dreadful news on the wireless. Malaya and Singapore had fallen, Rangoon and Mandalay were in flames. Nothing cheerful or hopeful.

I felt sure the Japanese would be in Maymyo soon and decided Ann that they would not have you. I decided I would drown you in the bath. I have often wondered if I ever could have done such a dreadful thing.

It was later that night that Mollie discovered she and Ann had been completely left behind – the pregnant mothers had departed shortly after the earlier group, at about 4 p.m.; somehow, they had been forgotten. But not for long. Salvation, of sorts, came with the arrival of Company Sergeant Major Birdsall, who was carrying out checks of the houses to make sure no one had been left. He was shocked to discover then that his own family were still in the camp, in addition to Mollie and Ann. Immediately, transport was arranged for both families, beginning with a journey in a 'gharry' which was, in Mollie's words: 'A dreadful thing. It was a box on four wheels pulled by a horse that was skin and bone. It was driven by a corporal.'

Mollie and Ann were forced to squeeze inside the box, together with Mrs Birdsall and her three children – Joyce who was 12, Raymond, 11 and Lorna, just 5. Also in the box were all of their belongings: mostly clothes, Ann's potty and a surgical shoe for Mollie. After a short, bumpy and uncomfortable ride in the gharry, they arrived at Maymyo railway station. Discomfort was about to become the order of the day. Mollie wrote:

It was packed with Burmese, Indians and Chinese with their goods, anything they could carry. We seemed to be the only Europeans. The noise was dreadful, everyone shouting. At last a train arrived, now it was murder, so much pushing. Our escorts found seats for us and at 1.15 am we were away.

What a journey! We were in a 3rd class compartment (never normally used by Europeans). The seats and back-rest were wooden laths. We had a bench affair which seated five so Mary Birdsall had Lorna on her knee. I nursed you, and Joyce, Raymond and our bundles were between us. We were packed like sardines. All the seats were full and every inch of the floor was covered with people squatting. The windows were blocked by people hanging on from the outside. There were no fans or toilets. Your potty came in useful for the Birdsall children as well as you. Mary and I were uncomfortable but managed to control ourselves, like 'Pukka Mem-Sahibs!' (a Hindi expression meaning 'absolute gentle women').

Mollie describes in her letter how she – together with the other 'sardines' – uncomfortably bumped along on this train for thirteen hours, hungry, thirsty, dirty and, for most of the time, dying to 'spend a penny'. Eventually Mollie reached a station and, together with Ann and the Birdsalls, disembarked and was 'rescued' by an RAF officer who offered to take them to an evacuee camp he knew of that was a couple of hours away.

The camp, marking the next stage of her journey to India – but this time a static leg because they were not moving – was at a place called Shwebo, a smallish town in the north of Burma with an airfield, around which rice plants were abundant. About 200 refugees, as which they now could be defined too, had arrived at the camp before Mollie and her small party. She described it as a dumping ground: rows and rows of beds covered in the clothes and belongings of people who were there at that moment, but also the belongings of some who had moved on but had not been able to take everything they owned for the next stage of their journey.

Upon arrival they had to report to an office and were given tickets that entitled them to a bed – which was more a case of finding what they could, amongst the chaos. Fortunately, they found mattresses to push together, after which their next search was for something to eat. Mollie wrote about the welcome meal they then had, which was tinned soup, meat and fruit. This meal was very important, however, because there was not enough food at the camp for all the evacuees at all, and hunger soon set in. The meagre supplies that Mollie and Mary Birdsall had brought with them were stolen, as were some of their (few) belongings. Mollie wrote:

Both mine and your clean dress were taken, as were my undies. Mary also lost several items of clothing. I was now left only with what I was wearing plus one shoe and you only had one dress and two pairs of pants. This was bad enough but when we found our food had been taken we felt it was a really mean thing to do. I only had soup, cheese biscuits, milk and four bars of chocolate – certainly not enough for two of us for very long. There was nothing we could do except pool what food we had left, tighten our belts and hoped our time there would be short …

Their stay at Shwebo lasted, in the end, for ten days; by the end Mollie wrote they were painfully hungry, only getting a little bit of food from an old man who passed by the camp and would sell them eggs, stale bread, tomatoes and mangoes. They were fed in the camp, but there was simply not enough to go round. Food bought from the man was a small added extra. All the time, too, the dangers of war became more evident with the sound of air raids and enemy aircraft overhead. Mollie recalled one especially frightening moment:

The planes were always very high. They took no notice of us and flew on which was just as well as there were no shelters or trenches. One afternoon we were strolling around when this alarm sounded. We decided to make towards a clump of trees. Once again we could see the planes as specks in the sky. Suddenly from nowhere, so it seemed, came a plane flying low shooting a machine-gun right across the camp. We threw ourselves to the ground. I laid over you, Ann. This you did not approve of – you really did yell. The plane had gone and I was just about to get up when I noticed a young RAF fellow crawling towards us telling me to 'stay put' as the plane would be back. He was right. I said we would be alright and he should go back to his troops; but he stayed with us. He protected us both.

I felt sorry for him because he told me afterwards he had lost both of his parents in a bombing raid, in England.

This, however, was not even the lowest moment for Mollie during their visit to the camp in Shwebo. In her letter, she recalled the day she learnt that the whole country of Burma had fallen into occupied Japanese hands. She said:

Each day on the notice board would be a list of names of the people who would leave on the next plane that arrived. The planes came at any old time. It was a case of when a plane landed, those concerned made their way to it and were away very quickly. On the eighth day our names were on the list. All day we waited but, instead of a plane coming to take us away we were given the grim news that Burma had capitulated, the Japanese had taken over. I cannot explain how we felt. We were also told there was little hope of more planes coming. If they did they might be intercepted on the way out. We had to decide if we wanted to return to our homes or stay there and hope for the best. Many people left the camp. We were the only Europeans left and very few others remained. It was difficult to know what to do, Mary and I talked about it for ages. We were hungry, thirsty and dirty. Food and water were scarce. In fact neither Mary nor I had eaten for 3 days or drunk for 2. You children had little. It was awful to hear you say 'Mummy, I'm hungry.' We would put you off for as long as we could and then try and make a little go a long way.

After many discussions we, that is Mary and I, decided to stay at the camp. If the Japanese wanted us they would have to come to us, we would not go to them.

However, two days later an aeroplane did arrive; Mollie, Ann and the Birdsalls had little choice but to board it. Mollie described the aircraft as 'fairly comfortable, we sat on a sort of thin bench around the inside, with dents which we sat on'.

After the plane departed, they drew some comfort from a male member of the crew – whose job it was to give out sick bags – because he was Chinese. But they thought the pilot was Japanese, and they had no idea where they were going. It was, in the end, just a two-hour journey, after which they landed in Bangladesh, much to their relief, in a town called Chittagong.

There followed a time of comfort for the two mothers and children alike. Bangladesh had not come under attack by the Japanese, and was an important Allied country used by the British as a front-line military base more and more as the war in the Pacific progressed. In complete contrast to their previous days, they were driven from Chittagong airfield by truck to the local golf club, where the expatriate community was enjoying a dinner dance.

The ladies and gentlemen at the dance were dressed in their finery; and when Mollie and her party arrived, she wrote:

Everyone looked our way. We must have looked a very sorry sight, talk about chalk and cheese. Here we were, dirty, smelly women and children and they were immaculate. Much to my surprise I heard 'there's Mollie Birch.' It was a lady I had met on the ship on my journey to Burma, four years before.

Before the next stage of their journey by train and ship, again not knowing where they were going, they were given clean clothes, baths and delicious food. Never was such kindness more needed, or more welcome. Circumstances were soon to force the two families, who by now had become very close, to go their separate ways; Mollie and Ann had not yet come through their most frightening time.

However, before the families' parting, and sustained by their hearty meal, Mollie, Ann and the Birdsalls embarked on a fairly brief but comfortable train journey, which, annoyingly because it interrupted welcome sleep, ended in the middle of the night because the train broke down. All the passengers had to disembark and begin a long, tiresome walk to a harbour (of sorts), including up a bank, which would have been especially hard for Mollie; but eventually they reached the paddle steamer that was waiting for them.

The steamer was docked in a small port, next (quite possibly, although not confirmed in Mollie's writing) to the shores of the Padma River, which is one of Bangladesh's most important waterways, a tributary to the far larger River Ganges. Mollie wrote of how crowded it was on the ship, but it was not an unenjoyable part of their journey:

> Ann, you had two choices: to stand or squat, but where you were you stayed. We moved away slowly and once again we did not know where we were going. To me it seemed a very wide river because, most of the time, although we could see land either side, it was in the far distance. It was not a bad ship, and it was a beautiful day and we were in the fresh air. We ate biscuits and chocolate and drank from water bottles given to us at the club.

After a few hours the ship came to a halt at a 'shaky jetty', and the passengers then had no choice but to disembark and scramble up a high bank, which revealed a railway line and a long, hot, exhausting wait – surrounded by many other people, all equally confused, exasperated and thirsty – before a train eventually stopped, which they boarded. Finally – though not the end of their journey by any means – this was the 'leg' of their journey which took them to India. Mollie wrote:

Now on another train, after eating more biscuits and drinking more water, we settled down to sleep. Lorna and Raymond shared the top bunk, Mary and you the lower, Joyce in a chair and me on the floor with my bundle as a pillow. Believe me, we all slept soundly. The next day every time the train stopped we looked for the name of the station. Early evening we arrived at Calcutta where we decided to leave the train. We went to a Military Policeman who escorted us to the Railway Transport Officer who, in his turn, sent us away in staff cars to Fort William. We had been wondering how we would get past the ticket collector because we had travelled from Burma to India by train, boat and train, again, without tickets.

Fort William was a garrison town surrounded by a high wall on the outskirts of Calcutta. I understand it was built as a fortress in case of riots. The British families would be safe in there with the gates closed and guarded. Once again we had to report to an office where we were told they were over-crowded with refugees, there was not a spare bed but they would see what they could do. They said we would be all right the following night as the next day many people would be moving to other places in India. First of all we were given a light meal and then taken to a very crowded barrack block. We were taken to a large room with one single bed. At one end of the bed lay a very old lady and, at the other, a young lady with a tiny baby. The floor was covered with women and children, there didn't appear to be room for anyone else. However, our escort moved a few people around, and a place was made for me to sit in a corner which was lucky because I could rest against the wall.

So, with you on my lap, we spent our first night in Calcutta, not comfortable but nice to be with British people again. Mary and her family were on the floor in another room.

The next day offered the two families some more welcome relief as many people left the fortress on coaches, but Mollie did not know where they were going. She wrote of their joy of being able to wash, have space to move around, and once again to have food and not be hungry.

However, during the night – perhaps just when, in theory, because of their improved circumstances things should have been starting to look up for them – Ann suddenly became ill and was hospitalised, suffering with dysentery. Sadly, for Mollie and Ann, the Birdsalls joined the exodus of evacuees leaving Fort William and it was not long, Mollie wrote, before she was the only woman left.

Ann was in hospital for three weeks, unconscious for much of the time and without her mother because Mollie had to stay at the fort. It was a lonely and anxious time for Mollie; but again, she drew comfort from where she could, and she recalled the compassion shown to her by the Indians. She wrote:

The staff were kindness itself to me, they lent me an iron and shoe brushes. Every morning there would be a knock on my door and a cup of tea on the step. For the first few days when I visited the hospital I saw you, but you did not see me. The hospital was a long way from the Fort, so I used to have a taxi most of the time.

It was also during this time – these long three weeks of Ann's illness – that Mollie was surprised and overjoyed by another unexpected happening. The 'hiking' party who had left Maymyo before they had arrived at the camp; the first Mollie knew of their being there was when she was woken up by one of the hikers squeezing her arm, saying, 'Mollie Birch! Hello, Mollie Birch!'

Finally, after Ann's recovery was assured, she and Mollie were able to leave Fort William for their next destination – not alone this time, but with some of their closest friends from Maymyo. By this time they had been travelling for seven weeks.

Their destination was 'Sabathu', an army hill station in the Simla Hills in northern India. Sabathu, Mollie wrote, was 'small but very pretty,' and had been specially created for evacuees from Burma, Malaya and Singapore.

Settling in Sabathu, initially, was difficult. Being a hill station, the access to their accommodation was, quite literally, up a steep hill and Mollie recalled how exhausted Ann, particularly, was upon having to climb to just reach the accommodation they were provided with. Mollie could not carry her daughter, both by now depleted of energy, so she smacked her and gave her no choice but to walk up the hill. Ann told me afterwards how they both cried when they reached the top.

The flat they were given by the army was one in a block they shared with their friends. It was, Mollie wrote:

Very nice; it had two bedrooms, a living room, kitchen, pantry, bathroom and toilet. A veranda ran all around the block like the deck of a ship, and we nick-named it the 'Queen Mary!'

However, once settled, the wives began to think of their menfolk, Mollie included. They needed their husbands urgently, not only for emotional reasons but for practical support too; a shortage of money became their next problem. Gradually most of the wives were able to locate their husbands with the help of the General Head Quarters army office in Delhi and couples and families were slowly reunited – and many, once together again, returned to England.

Mollie was, however, one of the last wives to be reunited with her husband Fred, during which time she worried very much about money; her friends were kind and offered to help but she wrote that she was too proud to accept their offers, until she almost had nothing. She wrote that it was at this time she felt the 'most depressed', and it was at this time, too, she lost her faith in God.

However, Mollie continued to try to locate Fred by letter, including asking him for funds, and she had written to her parents back in England. She recalled that one day, not long after sending these letters, she received separate replies to both within moments, with £100 from Fred and £40 from her parents. She wrote of the 'peace' this gave her, saying:

> I very humble and ashamed to think I had turned my back on God. After praying we would arrive somewhere safe and sound, a wish he had granted, at the last hour I had lost faith in him. It taught me a lesson.
>
> When you get to the stage of feeling you can't take any more don't lose faith, pray harder – it will all sort itself out in the end.

Two weeks after receiving some money, and being more comfortable, Mollie wrote:

> Your father arrived in Sabathu and, after 10 months, we were together again. He then had a month's leave before leaving us again. Our friend Mrs Butler, Lil, returned to England and we settled down for a quiet life. We were there for four years. Your father visited as often as he could and we visited him, too, at various places in India, including Calcutta where he was the Railway Transport Officer.
>
> This time when we went to Calcutta we went as the Major's family, not refugees.

★★★

India was an important, and reliable, ally for the British during the Second World War, providing the Allies with not only industrial, financial and military assistance – in the form of equipment – but most of all manpower; over 2½ million Indians (including many from Pakistan and Bangladesh) supported the Allied war effort, around 87,000 losing their lives. There was one attempt by the Japanese to invade India, in 1944, but it achieved very little. After the war ended, India emerged as the world's fourth-largest industrial power, its newfound strength paving the way for its independence from the United Kingdom in 1947.

Burma, on the other hand, continued to suffer through most of the Second World War because of the occupation by Japan. The Burma campaign was the only land campaign by the Allies in the Pacific that continued throughout the whole of the war; and for much of the time even Allied unity came under strain because the British, the Americans and the Chinese – despite being Allies – had opposing strategic priorities.

However, in 1944, the military tide began to turn; the Allies became stronger as the Japanese faltered. Finally, in May 1945, Burma's largest city, Rangoon – in the south – was liberated after over three years of occupation. The rest of the country followed and the Allies were able claim a costly, but hugely significant, victory.

Mollie Birch, *c.* 1995.

★★★

It was in 1945, too, that Mollie, Fred and Ann returned to England. In 2004, two years after Mollie died, Ann returned to Maymyo where she visited the railway station, the garrison church, the Roman Catholic Church – where she had been christened – and the gates of the army camp, which are now Burmese.

Ann collected some soil which she placed in a matchbox, and when she came home to England she placed the soil in her mother's grave. Mollie herself had never been able to return to Burma, so, in Ann's words, 'A little bit of Burma came to Mollie'.

NOTES

1   Victoria Panton Bacon, *Remarkable Journeys of the Second World War*, The History Press, 2020
2   Will Iredale, *The Kamakazi Hunters: Fighting for the War in the Pacific*, 1945, Macmillan, 2015

LEE EDWARDS:
A GERMAN JEWISH CHILD
WHO ESCAPED ON A
KINDERTRANSPORT TRAIN

Shards of glass littered Lee Edwards' home after the Nazis 'visited' her family during the night on 9 November 1938. She was 14 years old (nearly 15) at the time, and asleep in her bed when she was suddenly woken by her mother crying and the noise of windows being smashed as their beautiful home, on a leafy Frankfurt street, came under attack.

However, none of the damage the soldiers of Hitler's Reich wreaked upon young Lee's home that evening compared to what they did that was most devastating. This was the night she saw her father being dragged from the bed under which he was hiding and taken, terrified, and thrown into a crowded truck parked outside their home; one of many men suddenly becoming a prisoner, whose only 'crime' was that they were Jewish.

This is Lee's painful recollection of Kristallnacht,[1] also known as the 'Night of Broken Glass'. Her family home was one of thousands of Jewish homes, businesses, synagogues and schools torched and vandalised by the Nazis that night; over 100 Jews were killed and over 30,000 men were taken to concentration camps, including over 2,500 from Frankfurt

alone. This wave of anti-Jewish violence was unleashed all over Germany as well as in parts of annexed Austria, Poland and Czechoslovakia.

Lee Edwards, aged 14.

Lee, named Liesel by her parents Moritz and Sophie Carlebach, was born in Frankfurt just before Christmas in 1923. Of her childhood, Lee told me:

I was an extremely fortunate child for the first ten years or so of my life; my parents were 'well to-do', we had plenty of money because my father's business was successful; I went to a good school, I had my own nanny, and we had lots of Jewish friends.

But in 1933 when Hitler came to power things started to change for us. The changes were slow at first, but for five years things gradually got harder and harder, just because we were Jews. There were signs by the public parks and swimming pools, for example saying 'no entry to Jews' and I remember too the same signs outside restaurants, and the opera house.

I also felt sad because many of our Jewish friends left Germany; most went to America and some to China, but we couldn't leave because of my elder brother, Emil. He was ten years older than me, and 'idealistic'. Emil joined the communist party, and at the beginning of 1934 he was taken prisoner for distributing anti-Nazi propaganda. He was sentenced to three years in prison; at least he survived, but he was not released until the war ended in 1945.

So, because of Emil my parents and I did not leave Germany, and we were there for Kristallnacht.

Lee told me she has never forgotten seeing her father being taken away that night. She told me how fond she was of him, and that she was proud of him too because he had received an Iron Cross award for courageous action in the First World War. She said that for the first five years of Hitler's rule, after he came to power in 1933, her father continued to believe that future elections would reverse the damage Hitler was doing. 'But,' she said:

My father came home again after about a month of being held at Buchenwald prison. He returned a broken man, both physically and mentally. He had been beaten terribly, but what really crushed his spirit was knowing his country had turned against him.

Second World War historians, over the years since Hitler came to power, have presented several theories as to what it was that drove him, and the Nazi party he led, to loathe the Jews so much that they were able to inflict torture and devastation on the incomprehensible scale that they did. Perhaps one of the most likely theories is that Hitler – completely unfairly – blamed the Jews, as well as the communists, for Germany's defeat in the First World War.[2] Hitler himself had fought patriotically for Germany, so much so that he earned the same Iron Cross award that Lee's father had. Possibly Hitler felt let down after Germany surrendered in November 1918. At the time of the Armistice, he was in hospital suffering temporary blindness and other injuries. After his health began to improve, he wrote, 'When I was confined to bed, the idea came to me that I would liberate Germany, that I would make it great. I knew immediately it would be realised.' According to the Nazis, expelling the Jews was the solution to the problems in Germany.

Hitler was also infuriated by the Treaty of Versailles, which was the 1919 Peace Treaty that brought an end to the war between Germany and Allied powers. The Treaty forced Germany to accept the blame for bringing about the First World War and imposed harsh punishment, including giving away parts of German territories to other countries, financial penalties and a weakened military. The treaty – indeed, the whole aftermath of the First World War – left Germany in a state of chaos and many political groups sprang up, rebelling against each other.

As Hitler's physical strength returned, he grew in determination and entered politics as a member of the German Workers' Party. He vowed to make Germany 'economically strong again' and was elected in 1932 as leader of the National Socialist German Workers' Party (the official name of the Nazi party). He was appointed Chancellor in January 1933. An Act followed, called The Enabling Act, which ensured Hitler was able to rule Germany as the dictator he became.

The life changes for the Carlebach family, and thousands of other Jewish families besides – as Lee explained – were not hugely dramatic in the early days of Hitler coming to power, but as the weeks and months progressed the laws he passed had more and more impact on their daily lives, eroding their quality of life and instilling fear. Jewish families such as the Carlebachs were living in a state of uncertainty and oppression after Hitler came to power and before Kristallnacht, but I wonder if many realised that Hitler's aim was complete control, at all costs. Who would have thought, even then, that just a few years later a 'Holocaust' would come to pass, taking the lives of over 6 million European Jews?

Jewish children like Lee in these countries also had to be 'dealt with'. As mentioned earlier, many Jewish families did manage to leave these countries when they realised their safety was compromised; but many did not: the Carlebachs, because of Emil's imprisonment, are one example, but far more would not have been able to afford to leave and would not have had anywhere to go. Travel visas were also difficult to obtain.

Many children had no option but to go into hiding, but for others there was, however, a 'rescue'. It was far from ideal because it separated them from their parents (most families were never reunited), but it was a system that did save the lives of over 10,000 Jewish children in Germany, Austria, Poland and Czechoslovakia, including that of Lee Edwards. This rescue system was a British scheme called *Kindertransport*.[3] Lee said:

I didn't want to leave my family, but when my mother found out that trains were being arranged to take children to places of safety in the United Kingdom, she registered for me to go. I wasn't even going to school after Kristallnacht – it had closed because most of the teachers had been taken too or had escaped.

I learnt after the war, from Emil, that he had actually met up with my father in Buchenwald prison in November 1938; Emil had told him that if they could, they must send me away, because otherwise I would highly likely be killed.

I don't remember very much about my journey to England; I do remember, however, my father waving at me from the window of our home, and my mother crying, wiping her eyes with a handkerchief. I and the other children had labels around our necks with numbers on them, instead of names, and the Germans made sure we didn't have anything we weren't allowed. But my mother had given me a necklace, a really precious necklace made of pearls and diamonds that the Nazis didn't find. I still have it today.

After leaving Germany we travelled through Holland and got to The Hague, and I do remember that there we were given cheese sandwiches and cocoa. Then we got on a boat and travelled to Harwich. The customs officers there saw my necklace, but they didn't take it away. Then we all took a train to Liverpool Street station. I didn't know then I would never see my parents again. I learnt after the war that my father committed suicide shortly after I left, and I never found out how or when my mother died.

Kindertransport was the informal name given to this extensive rescue operation, initiated by the British government. Speaking in the House of Commons, shortly after the atrocities of Kristallnacht, Home Office Minister Samuel Hoare MP said, 'Here is a chance of taking the young generation of a great people, here is a chance of mitigating to some extent the terrible suffering of their parents and friends.' There followed a vote which supported a motion to allow a then unspecified number of refugee children under the age of 17 into the United Kingdom. It was agreed to admit the children on temporary travel documents with the idea that they would rejoin their parents when the crisis was over. Sadly, however, because of the Holocaust that was a reality for very few of the children who boarded the trains; Lee Edwards was one of many children left an orphan as a result.

Kindertransport was unique, too, in that it was made possible because religious groups came together in a way that they had not done so before – Jews, Quakers and Christians of many denominations, funded by wealthy British benefactors, including the Hoare family, Lord Baldwin (Prime Minister between the two world wars) and Sir Nicholas Winton. The first train left on 1 December 1938, bringing 196 Jewish children who were previously living at an orphanage in Berlin that was burnt down by the Nazis on 9 November 1938. The last 'official' *Kindertransport* train departed on 1 September 1939, two days before the Second World War began; but one final journey was arranged for eighty children in Holland who were given refuge in the United Kingdom on 14 May 1940, as the Netherlands was falling into occupied hands.

Parents of many of the children in the persecuted countries were able to arrange in advance, with the organisers of *Kindertransport*, where their children would stay. But it was not the case for all of them, so a 'camp' was set up for refugee children who arrived in the UK but had no onward destination, which provided them with a place of safety whilst they waited for a family to come forward to volunteer to take them in. Many of the refugee children would not have seen each other again after beginning their 'new lives' with their new families because they were scattered all over the British Isles in foster homes, in cities, on farms and some were placed in existing children's homes. Most of the 10,000 children found themselves in happy, welcoming homes provided by kindly families who despaired for the appalling circumstances the evacuees had fled from – but it was not the case for all, inevitably.

Perhaps, in some ways, it was hardest for the eldest children because, unfortunately, a number of these children were invited into British homes to live, but also to work. Such was the case for Lee.

Lee Edwards (then Liesel Carlebach) was just 15 years and 3 months old when she boarded the train from Frankfurt. She said:

I knew nothing at all about the family I was going to stay with, except they lived in a city called Coventry, and I was going to stay with a young Jewish couple called Mr and Mrs Harris. When I arrived, I realised Mrs Harris was pregnant; they wanted, and needed a 'home help' – that was me.

They were kind but I was extremely disappointed because I wanted to go to school and carry on learning. I was a good student back at my school in Frankfurt, I had worked hard, and I know I was quite bright, and my parents had high hopes for me. But because of the war and everything changing I didn't ever receive a proper education or go to university.

But I can see now, looking back, I had an education of a quite different type. Their first child was born in August 1939, so I was in a house with a tiny newborn baby; so, I learnt not only domestic cleaning skills but also about babies. I didn't realise it at the time because I was so upset not being able to go to school, but now I realise that this family taught me important life lessons, such as how to stand on my own two feet, and how to be organised, which helped me later on when I worked in an office.

I didn't make a lot of friends, but I did have one friend who lived nearby who was a '*Kindertransport*' child too – she had been in the same class as me at school! At the time I thought she was lucky, she had gone to a wealthy family; I went to her house once a week for tea, which we drank out of china cups. It all felt unfair because I felt I was 'making a lot of beds', whereas she would have treats like fish and chips. But saying all of that, in the end I was the more fortunate one because the parents in the family she was staying with broke up and my friend became very unhappy.

When I had been with the Harrises for about a year and half their house was destroyed by a bomb and they were evacuated to Wales. They kindly offered for me to go with them, but I didn't want to because I wanted to learn – so I stayed behind with a local teacher who took me in. I didn't go to school because she wanted domestic help too, but at her home at least I was able to learn shorthand and I managed to learn French too.

However, in the relatively short time Lee was with the Harrises, she grew very fond of their baby, a little boy called Tony. A lovely outcome for her is that she has kept in touch with the Harris family, and she is still in contact with Tony today. He is now 81 years old, has had a career as a dentist and lives in Liverpool. Tony kindly agreed to speak to me too, and of Lee he said:

> Lee is a wonderful lady; I can't speak highly enough of her. My parents thought so too, we have all kept in touch over the years. I lost touch myself as I was growing up, but she visited my parents in Wales after I got married, when I was in my 20s, and I loved seeing her again. Since then, we have met up on a number of occasions, both here and in Los Angeles. We speak about once a month now, and when she answers the telephone Lee still says, 'Hello Tony, my baby!' Lee is a small, incredible lady whom I am so fortunate to know.

Tony continued to explain that he and his parents had to leave Coventry because the house they lived in, in Queen Victoria Road, was destroyed during the Blitz, in November 1940. He recalled how his parents lost almost everything; they went to Bridgend in Wales because that was where his mother's parents lived. He spoke of the way his mother, especially, was traumatised and how difficult it was for them in Wales because – before finding a house to rent – the three of them lived in one small room. However, Tony also remembers the men who worked as hard as they could in gardens throughout Bridgend, particularly in the latter war years. 'Guess who they were,' he said to me. 'German prisoners of war!'

Understandably, however, Lee also told me that as the war progressed thoughts of her family were rarely far from her mind. She said that after arriving in England in March 1939 she did have some contact with her mother, but almost all communication stopped with the outbreak of the war in September. The last letter Lee received from her mother was sent in May 1942, written to Lee shortly before her deportation (and sent to her via the Red Cross). Her mother wrote: 'Dear Liesel, I am emigrating; hope to keep writing. Perfectly healthy and calm. You stay the same, be positive … sincere kisses, Mother.'

Lee learned after the war that her home in Frankfurt, probably shortly after she left for England, had become a *Judenhaus* – i.e. somewhere that quite a large number of Jews would have been forcibly interned (including her mother). She did not learn of her father's death until after the war; her brother, Emil, was able to tell her what happened to him, after they were \d in 1946. Lee told me it has been a 'comfort' to her, over the years, to at least know what happened to her father, but even more that he has a proper grave at the Jewish cemetery in Frankfurt, which she has visited over the years during her visits to Germany.

Emil, Lee told me, emerged from his eleven years of captivity absolutely committed to the communist cause. The Nazi concentration camp where he had been held for eight years was at Buchenwald near Weimar in the centre of Germany. It was one of the Nazi's earliest and largest camps, holding Jewish prisoners from all over Europe, as well as other inmates who were mentally ill, disabled or homosexual. Most of the prisoners were forced to work in local factories or on the railway line, and insufficient food, poor conditions, and deliberate executions led to the deaths of over 50,000 of its detainees.

However, despite the physical hardship of such a long internment, Emil Carlebach, after the war, proved he had inherited his father's work ethic. Far from being beaten by the 'system' he began a successful career in the newspaper industry and was a founding member of one of Germany's most successful newspapers, the *Frankfurter Rundschau*, a socialist publication within which he was able to express his views. Emil Carlebach was born in Frankfurt in 1914 and died there, too, in 2001, aged 87 years. Lee said:

> Of course, everything that had happened to him after Hitler came to power, and during the war, changed him, how couldn't it? He was always strong-willed as a child, but after the war he was an embittered man, a die-hard communist. We went our separate ways eventually, but we did stay in touch – I had my heart set on going to America (I just wanted to be able to eat nice things like tinned peaches!), but Emil wanted to stay in Europe; he lived mostly in Germany and spent some time in Paris. He had a good, long life, getting married and had a daughter, Amina. Amina has died now, I am leaving the necklace to her daughter, Lena. Not having children of my own I am glad to have a great-niece to give it to.

★★★

After the war ended, Lee Edwards – now in her early 20s – returned to Germany and found a secretarial job in the American Occupation Army, located in Esslingen near Stuttgart. It was an ideal position for her, not least because of her linguistic skills – she had knowledge of French as well as being fluent in English and German. But most importantly this is where she met her husband, Jimmy, also a German Jewish refugee.

Jimmy left Berlin in 1934 aged 21 and came to England. In 1939, shortly after war was declared, he joined the British Army and, amongst many other duties, supported the Allies during the evacuation of Dunkirk in 1940 and participated in D-Day in 1944. When he and Lee met, in Esslingen, his family name was Eckhaus (meaning 'corner house'), but for reasons of safety (effectively to counter threats from Neo-Nazism) they made the decision to Anglicise their name, changing it to Edwards – which they were entitled to do because Jimmy had served in the British Armed Forces.

Lee and Jimmy married in Frankfurt in 1947 and settled there for a while, which was an important time for Lee especially, because not only was she just married, but it also gave her precious to time to spend with Emil – which she had, of course, completely missed out on over the previous eleven years.

However, apart from Emil, there was little reason for the newly wedded Mr and Mrs Edwards to stay in Frankfurt. Their dream was to make a home for themselves in America. Their next hurdle was the visa challenge – it was difficult to emigrate directly to America from Germany in the early post-war years, so – instead – they went to Vancouver, in Canada, where they lived for three years. Finally, in 1950 their visas for America came through and Lee and

Jimmy moved to Los Angeles, where they quickly settled, Jimmy working as an accountant and Lee as a secretary. Lee said:

Because we didn't have children it was quite easy for us to travel back to Europe, which we did quite often; so over the years I did see Emil and his family, and Tony, and we would visit my father's grave. Jimmy died in 2005. We were so lucky to have each other.

Lee and her husband Jimmy, *c.* 1945.

Lee with her great-niece Lena Sarah
Carlebach, 2017.

★★★

This chapter ends with a couple of short but poignant quotes: words that
belong to Rabbi Shlomo Carlebach, to whom Lee is related. Shlomo
Carlebach was born in 1925 and died in 1994, during which time he was
well known in the European Jewish community for his writing, poetry,
songwriting and inspiring public speaking. Amongst many other comforting and uplifting words, he said: 'There are no tears without joy; and there
are no joys without tears;' and 'Love cannot be taught. All we can hope for
is that maybe we can unlearn all the hatred. Because hatred is taught. Love
is from Heaven.'

NOTES

1 'Kristallnacht' in *Holocaust Encyclopedia* (ushmm.org), United States Holocaust
   Memorial Museum
2 www.annefrank.org/en/anne-frank/go-in-depth/why-did-hitler-hate-jews
3 www.kindertransport.org

GALINA BROK-BELTSOVA: A RUSSIAN AVIATOR WHO FLEW ON THE FRONT LINE FOR THE RED ARMY

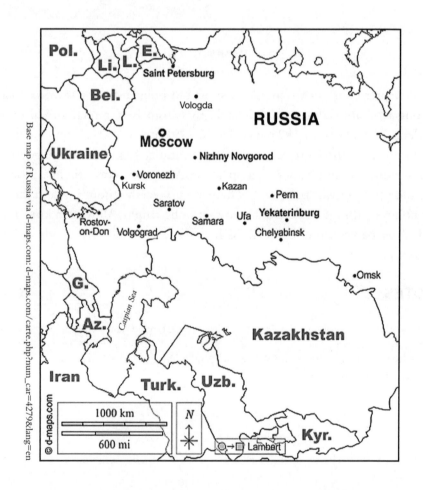

The month is October. The year is 1941. The location is Moscow. Our remarkable woman is Galina Brok-Beltsova; she is only 16 years old. It is cold; biting winds from the east have arrived, reminding the Muscovites of the bitter winter that is yet to come. However, they have more to fear than harsh weather. Their city is under threat; the three-month Battle of Moscow began at the beginning of the month, during which time many Soviet citizens would be killed, fearfully wounded, taken prisoner, or never found again.

'When the bombs started to fall,' Galina said:

We were overwhelmed. The enemy invaded very suddenly, so much so that we knew we needed to do something. We had no fear because we did not know the war. But we learnt because when in the morning if you walk down your lane and at night a bomb has dropped and you lose your school friend, and that friend never comes back to class, you become angry. Very angry. So you want to fight back. And fighting back is precisely what I, Galina Brok, did.

In her mid-teens, together with all her friends in the tenth grade at Moscow School Number Three, she took her first steps, 'thinking of the victory'. She described the decision to go to war, and not stay away from it, as something inevitable because of her devotion to her country. She told me how immensely grateful she was for the 'great teaching' she had received at her school, which she loved and which, above all, had taught her to be patriotic. It is not by chance, I am sure, that the Russians do not refer to the war as the Second World War, or World War Two, but as the Great Patriotic War and The Holy War.

Russia – then the Union of Soviet Socialist Republic (USSR) – lost so much, and so many, during the Great Patriotic War. Galina Brok-Beltsova's truly remarkable story is representative of the women whom she fought alongside during the years of war, but she has also told it for far, far many more – for all Russians, both civilians and servicemen, who lost their lives. Of the staggering number who died, she said:

I am happy I can speak for the 27 million who died in the war, who cannot speak. It is very important to tell the truth about these times for future generations so that it will never happen again. We have to keep improving our forces and keep our attention on those who still want war. Immediately after the war we still had no less an important fight for the restoration of our country. It is still the same today. I know the Soviet Union made terrible things … but nevertheless if we try think it through and understand the past, we will have a safer future.

I know I have written, repeatedly, in this book about the strength that can be drawn from reading of the experiences of all our *Remarkable Women*. This point is perhaps more relevant for this chapter than any other. I am not saying Galina is any more 'remarkable' than our other women – they are all equally remarkable in their own way and for many different reasons – but I feel compelled to remind you of the strength you can draw from Galina, before I tell you her story, because as I think about it, I am drawing strength. Her sheer courage, and that of the women she fought alongside, is extraordinary; and – I think – as well as being inspiring, is utterly commendable.

Galina was one of over 1,000 female aviators who took the fight all the way to the front line, amongst some 800,000 women who served in the Red Army. (At some points during the war there were up to a million.) Thousands were nurses, and many others became accomplished and highly successful snipers, anti-aircraft gunners, signal and communications operators, drivers and train drivers; between them all, directly bringing about the deaths of hundreds of Germans. The aviators entered the war as pilots, navigators, gun-radio operators and ground crew. They were employed in three female combat units: the 586th Fighter Regiment, the 587th Dive Bomber Regiment (in which Galina served as a navigator) and the 588th Night Bomber Regiment, as well as in some male air-force regiments.[1]

So it was that Galina took to the sky, which was often freezing cold and busy with the enemy all around, accompanied only by her two crew members – both girls as young, but I expect every bit as courageous and determined, as she. By the time the war ended Galina was just 20 years and 3 months old – when she flew in combat the first time, she had just turned 19. The passing of over seventy-five years since the war ended has not dimmed her recall of her most dramatic moments including some during her first operation, and the time (almost certainly amongst others) she was convinced she would not return. Galina remembers:

I studied the maps so well before the flight. But after reaching the sky I couldn't find any of the villages, or forests – everything had been burned – the Nazis cut them down, destroyed all they could, fearing the partisans. It was really hard to navigate – after we luckily returned from the mission, I asked the 'old men' what to do in such a situation (we called 'old men' the girls from the regiment who had already been flying before we joined and they seemed to us highly experienced. Some people around were wondering why we called them 'old' as they were in their early 20s, and we would answer it was because they knew so much more). The 'old men' reassured me by saying everything would come with experience ... and they were right, and my further life experience proved it.

If ever there was a case of being 'thrown into the deep end', this was it. There was no such thing as a 'gentle introduction' to the war for these women, no 'allowances' were made to take account of their gender. This operation, Galina's first, was at the Western Front, part of the campaign to free Belarus (then known as the Soviet Socialistic Republic of Belarus, or BSSR) and parts of the Baltic republics. Belorussia (now Belarus), an Eastern European country about the same size as the United Kingdom, had been under German occupation since 1941; the (successful) liberation operation, called *Operation Bagration* – of which Galina was part – was launched in June 1944, freeing the Belorussians from the stranglehold of their Nazi occupiers, who had been relentlessly cruel. Nearly 400,000 Belarussian civilians during the occupation were deported for slave labour and hundreds of villages were destroyed; by the end of the occupation nearly 2 million Belorussians had been killed.[2]

Galina Brok-Beltsova, *c*. 1944.

Galina, as navigator, was seated in the cockpit of their Petlyakov Pe-2 dive bomber[3] aircraft, with her pilot, and was responsible for dropping the bombs, operating the 'Berezin' gun, protecting the aircraft from above, as well as giving directions. Theirs was just one of hundreds of Soviet aircraft (in addition to tanks and artillery on the ground) deployed during this extremely significant operation. It lasted for some nine weeks. The Soviets were forced to fight hard and it was costly – around 180,000 Soviet troops were killed or went missing, and the Red Army lost 2957 tanks, 2447 guns and mine-throwers, and 822 planes – but it did prove to be a decisive victory, paving the way for the final assault on Nazi Germany.

What an experience for a young girl to be part of such a significant turning point in Second World War history. In terms of the outcome of the whole of the war, Operation Bagration was no less important than another successful liberation operation achieved earlier that month, but further West and far better-known – I am referring, of course, to D-Day, and the beginning of the liberation of France and the Low Countries.

Galina recalled that during this, her first operation, not only could she not identify landmarks on her maps because they had been destroyed, it was also difficult to navigate because of the huge number of friendly and enemy aircraft in the sky with them; flying in formation, as they were, with many other Soviet aircraft. They would say, 'Such close quarters in the sky today;' some 6,000 planes were engaged in this operation. Perhaps strength in numbers, the feeling of being part of an extensive, determined team, would have been something of a comfort. She must have been frightened, but Galina didn't speak of this, or recall fear – rather giving me the feeling that adrenalin would have flowed furiously at every moment. She preferred to reflect too on her admiration of her flying machine – their Petlyakov Pe-2, which they called their 'Peshka' or 'Pawn'. It was, indeed, one of the Soviet's most outstanding tactical attack aircraft – small enough (about 17m wide and 13m long) to be able to gather considerable speed when it urgently needed to (powered by its two engines), but feisty enough to serve as a dive bomber, equally serviceable during night as well as daytime flights. (Likening it to a game of chess, because of the significance of its role this aircraft was written about in a book called *The Pawn that became the Queen*.)

It was during a different flight, however, some weeks later, that young Galina genuinely felt her demise was imminent. She said:

I can't remember where we were, but I can remember being in the air when all of a sudden one of our two engines started to hiccup and lost full throttle. We went to the back of the formation we were flying in, which was protected by the fighters, while the enemy attackers were fighting ahead of us. We could see the enemy fighters attacking the formation, and the gun shots blasting all around the formation ahead and all we could do was fly at the back and observe how our formation was manoeuvring to avoid gun blasts, and slowing down, hanging over the target areas for better accuracy of the bombing. We could see all that, but we couldn't do much with one powered-down engine. Then after dropping all the bombs the formation and all our escort fighters turned around and started heading back to the base, and I remember it went quiet and nothing, no aircraft at all were with us. We found ourselves to be alone in the clear sky with no enemy fighters or anti-aircraft gun shooting which allowed us to drop all our bombs and photograph destroyed targets undisturbed, flawlessly completing our mission. We had turned round and were flying home, feeling thrilled and happy because we completed the mission and it was completely empty sky, in bright sunshine, and we had dropped our bombs accurately.

Then, suddenly, there was a shout from our gunner at the back of the plane who said, 'They are back, two Focke Wulfes [German fighter aircraft] are coming for us.' Our aircraft had three guns – one pointed up, one down and one to the front – we shot from them, but our plane had a weak spot as it had blind shooting areas on the sides of the plane. Because of those blind areas we used our signal pistols from the cockpit windowpane, shooting at German fighters coming to the sides of our plane. This [measure] couldn't shoot down the fighter but sometimes we did manage to scare the pilot [fighter] off. At first Germans even took it for some kind of new weapon used against them. The German pilots were aware of the weakness in our shooting range and one of the Germans came right alongside us and pointed at us. He showed us one finger and then two asking with how many shots we would prefer him to send us down. He could have done anything. I remember feeling angry, not scared. There was no point in being afraid. But they didn't do anything. Our brilliant pilot, Antonina Spitsina, dropped the plane down, up, left and right and suddenly it went quiet again, and I saw fighters with Red stars next to us on both sides, and then we were flying with some French pilots of Normandie-Niemen who had seen we were in trouble and came back to protect us and guide us back to the base.

On another occasion Galina was trapped in the body of her aircraft on the ground, after it had had to make an emergency landing. She said:

> A nearby aircraft collided with us while we were in the air, and tore off part of the tail of our plane. We couldn't continue flying but we still had our bombs on board. Landing with full bomb load is extremely dangerous and an emergency landing on the fighter's short airstrip is doubly dangerous. We needed to get rid of our bombs but we didn't know where to 'dump' because we were over our own advancing ground troops. But we did land, we had to, we landed on a field and fortunately our plane ran into sandy hill and came to a halt. The pilot and the gunner at the back got quickly out, but my legs were stuck by the emergency tank. The girls were shouting at me, 'Faster, there is fuel, bombs, what are you doing? Everything will explode ...' In the end, somehow I got out, and the plane didn't explode. We survived and it seemed necessary to rejoice but we couldn't.

Galina recalled too her disappointment that the body of their aircraft was broken and how upset they felt thinking their mission had not been accomplished; but what a vital lesson it was for her. It was after this emergency landing that Galina promised herself that she would try by all means to 'complete all matters immediately, not postponing anything until later'.

Whilst the majority of Galina's operations were undertaken by day, the women who flew in one of the two sister regiments, the 588th, flew at night and were so feared by the Germans they were nicknamed *Nachthexen* – Night Witches.

The 588th became the most highly decorated female force of the three aviation regiments, flying over 24,000 sorties in three years between May 1942 and May 1945, dropping over 3,000 tonnes of bombs and 26,000 incendiaries on invading German armies.[4] Their 'Night Witch' nickname came around in part because of the aircraft they flew in, a *Polikarpov U-2*, which is a wood and canvas open cockpit bi-plane that left the crew completely open to the elements, and one that could be flown very quietly on approach to its target – enabling the crew to successfully bomb the targets because they hadn't been seen, because the 'Night Witches' were able to fly so as to avoid light beams and anti-aircraft guns. The Germans feared and resented these women, particularly because they were effectively able to outwit them; the noise of their aircraft was likened by the Germans to the sound of a sewing machine, gently tapping away. In addition to the protection the Night Witches were afforded by being able to approach the enemy so quietly, the *Polikarpov*, seating just a crew of two (pilot and navigator, who very often would not even have parachutes), was so small it didn't show up on radar, and they didn't have radios either, so there were no signals to give them away. Speaking about her first combat mission over the front line in Ukraine, a pilot in the night bombers regiment, Nadezhda Popova said:[5]

> It seemed that it was an abyss of darkness, pitch black … and when I got up in the air, I could see the front line marked by green, red, and white tracer lights, where skirmishes continued throughout the night. We were trained to look for projector lights as we were used to flying blind in total darkness. A plane in front of me was suddenly illuminated and I witnessed its fatal descent. I flew towards the enemy lines, thinking I must help my friends. Irrational thoughts … I knew they were dead. We dropped the bombs on the dots of light below. The Germans shot at us and I circled round and flew back towards the base … I was ordered to fly another mission immediately. It was the best thing to keep me from thinking about it.

Preparation for the women in all the aviation regiments was equally tough; certainly no dispensation or extra comforts were provided because they were female. After signing up to join the Women's Red Army in 1942 and completing over a year of study as a meteorologist, Galina responded to the invitation to undergo training and apply for a role in one of the three aviation regiments, which were established in response to a direct request to Russian General Commander-in-Chief Joseph Stalin from Marina Raskova, who had already proven herself to be an accomplished pilot by breaking several world records of long-distance non-stop flights, her longest flight taking twenty-six hours and twenty-nine minutes – travelling from Moscow to the Sea of Orkhotsk in the east.

Raskova was well-known in Russia and had also earned the respect of Stalin who, therefore, responded positively to her suggestion that women should be trained up and employed as aircrew in the same way as men. After receiving permission to set up the regiments in 1941, Raskova took little time to recruit and train almost 1,000 women in the three different units –

herself leading Galina's regiment, the 587th. Galina respected her very much; Raskova was a skilled pilot and driven leader, but was equally admired for her kind-heartedness, sense of humour and sensitivity. She would sometimes sing to the recruits during breaks in their training. However, there were rules and orders had to be followed. Galina said:

> After being enrolled in the ranks of the Red Army, the first thing we all did was have our hair cut. This was the order of Marina Raskova. Nobody dared disobey. She said war was not the time for hairstyles. When the war ends, she said, 'you will have braids and curls'. We had a very strict and tight schedule and only five minutes to go to the bathhouse. There was no time to wash long hair. And always you'd get out of the plane all sweaty and dishevelled.

If it was chilly in Moscow in 1941 when the Battle of Moscow had began, it was far colder in Samara, a city some 1,000km south-east of the Russian capital, located near the banks of the mighty Volga River. This is where Galina – and many of her classmates – began their training for service in the Red Army. These young people, immensely loyal to their homeland, were communists in the making, all having been accepted into the army (though few were refused because so many were needed) after joining Komsomol – a Soviet patriotic youth organisation which was doing all it could to recruit as many members as possible. Membership of Komsomol at this time later granted them membership into the communist party. Reflecting on the time in October 1941 when she signed up, Galina said:

> Together with other Moscow plants and manufactures my father was evacuating his factory machines and equipment to the East where all his workers and their families were moved too. But there was no sign of panic, and there were cinemas in military Moscow. Whole classes attended lectures in cinemas where we went to learn about the war and what to do in case of an air raid. During one such session, an air raid was announced: everyone was evacuated to the subway, which was adapted as a bomb shelter. We went to the Semeonvskaya station, which was just being built. There were no escalators yet. We went down the wooden steps for about fifteen minutes, it seemed endless. And below, on the platform, there were old people, children and pregnant women.

We were all so shocked by seeing these vulnerable people being forced to hide like this that we all enlisted, without hesitation. We were overwhelmed with the desire to do at least something to bring victory closer. On every corner there were posters, saying such things as: 'How did you help the front?', 'Motherland calls', and 'Kill the enemy.' I can still see a 'toothy Fritz' on a poster with one of those propaganda materials in front of my eyes.

So their 'training' began – on the outskirts of a city previously unknown to them, for much of the time subjected to coping with temperatures as low as −30°C. Galina's 'new life' began in an inauspicious and extremely unexpected way:

All volunteers came from schools and universities but there was no living space, so – for us – we went to the stables, big bulky hangars – with layers and bunks for about 300 people and we slept on the mattresses made of pillowcases stuffed with straw. It was not unsanitary inside the heated warm barrack, but we first had to use the wooden summer toilet built outside in the yard. Then we found another room next to the stable, but the door to it was locked because of a big broken nail that had been banged into it. We pulled the nail out, opened the door and found a bathroom, divided into smaller sections, but it was extremely dirty with huge piles of fecal matter, frozen solid …

The same evening, our Commander lined us up and asked, 'Who dared open the shutdown room? Make three steps out of the line!' I stepped out of the line and took responsibility, and he said, 'From now on you, Galina Brok, are not a Private, you are a Lance Sergeant and my assistant, and everyone is under your command, and must take your orders as if they are mine.' He ordered me to walk ahead of the line. I was the youngest girl in the whole barrack to become the Platoon commander and became known as 'Young Commander'.

It was a year or so later that 'Young Commander' responded to the invitation to join one of Marina Raskova's three female aviation regiments – out of around 2,000 brave young women who applied, just over half were accepted. So it was that the next stage of Galina's Patriotic War journey began, learning the art of navigation at the 3rd Reserve air regiment in Yoshkar-Ola city, in Mari El Republic, which was situated along the northern bank of the River Volga. The girls, and men, had to learn in a few months what would normally take several years to grasp. The demands of the war would not wait …

Almost 2,000 women were trained up to be snipers to serve on the front line between 1941 and 1945; they had a high success rate but their success was accompanied by a high loss rate – only around a quarter of the women survived. They trained at the 'Central Women's School of Sniper Training', just outside Moscow; here they learnt to shoot using a 7.62mm bolt-action rifle – originally adopted by the Tsar's (Alexander III) army in 1891.

Of the most outstanding pupils was Lyudmila Pavlichenko[6] who 'sniped' 309 Nazis, killing all of them; her service on the front line, however, lasted for just under a year – beginning during the siege of Odessa (Ukraine) in June 1941, ending in June 1942 as the siege of Sevastapol (on the coast of the Black Sea, in the Crimea) was under way. This figure of 309 kills in a year does, of course, equate to almost one kill per day; but it doesn't work like that – there were days where she didn't kill at all, possibly the days she was 'counter-sniping', ie. surreptitiously spying on the enemy to establish their objectives. There were, almost certainly, however, days upon which she successfully 'sniped' more than one Nazi.

Pavlichenko's 'reign' on the frontline ended somewhat abruptly after she was struck in the face by a mortar shell; following which her evacuation (via submarine) was ordered by the Soviet High Command. After recovering, instead of returning to the frontline, she trained other young women and helped the Red Army with propaganda campaigns.

For her achievements, she received the accolade of the nickname 'Lady Death' because she was (and I expect still is) the most successful female sniper in recorded history. Pavlichenko was also awarded the 'Gold Star of the Hero of the Soviet Union' award in 1943, which is the highest military distinction she could have been given, in addition to receiving the 'Order of Lenin' twice – the highest civilian decoration bestowed by the Soviet Union. Pavlichenko is quoted as saying: 'We mowed down Hitlerites like ripe grain.'[7]

She was one of around ninety women who received the 'Hero of the Soviet Union' award for their service during the war; but only around six of these were given to the women snipers – the aviators received far more recognition, and Marina Raskova was one of around thirty who received this accolade. Her award was given posthumously – Raskova was killed in January 1943, after her aircraft crashed into a bank on the River Volga whilst she was flying in conditions of poor visibility. Indeed, Raskova's place in

Russian history was set to become legendary; she also received the first state funeral of the war and her ashes are buried in the Kremlin Wall.

However, how can anything be more bittersweet than praise for being a successful killer, even if it is known by the perpetrator that killing was a necessary evil, vital to secure the future of the Motherland? Pavlichenko, for example, could justify what she did – and be proud of herself – but what of peace of mind? I have read, unsurprisingly, that she suffered after the war with depression and post-traumatic stress (her state of mind not helped by her husband dying during the war), and she died relatively young – aged 58 – following a stroke, in 1974.

★★★

Galina's post-war history is, thankfully, somewhat happier; indeed hers is actually a beautiful and romantic story about love which endured, and through endurance, succeeded and gave life to so many. The love story began in 1942, whilst Galina – then sweet 17 – was learning the art of navigation, in Yoshkar-Ola city.

Georgy Beltsov was her commander; she recalled how she, and her fellow trainees, could not help but notice how striking Georgy was. Galina, however, kept her feelings to herself (at the beginning especially), not wanting to be distracted from what she urgently needed to learn to navigate successfully: 'I was focussed on going to the front. But he started to write me three letters a day.' (What could a young girl in this situation do, I ask myself as I write this? The situation for these girls was most unusual, as precarious and uncertain as any situation could possibly be. How could one think of love whilst one is being prepared for survival in the face of likely death?)

Georgy, however, as well as successfully commanding 'Young Commander' and the other female recruits, did not waiver in his conviction that he had found his future wife in Galina, and after training they kept in contact by writing to each other. Just before her first operation he made a point of finding Galina and presenting her with a photograph of a small white bear, writing the following words to her: 'This is our talisman. Please always carry this photo with you when you fly. It will keep you safe.' And after thirty-six operations – some of which could have gone either way – the war did, indeed, end safely for her.

After the war's end, whilst she was stationed in Lithuania, in Panevezis town, Captain Georgy Beltsov went to find her and asked her to marry him. Initially, she refused, dreaming of at last being able to continue her studies and wishing for university. However, the refusal was short-lived; partly because her friends supported her being with him, but mostly she realised the depth and truth of his affection, and was taken aback when he said, 'I waited the whole war for you. And you, now, with your soldier's boots, are tramping on the soul of a man who is devoted to you.' She recalled his trembling lips, and that he was on the verge of tears. 'It was,' she said, 'a cold shower that sobered me up and made me change my mind.'

They had a thrifty wedding soon after becoming engaged, and their union lasted sixty years, ending upon Georgy's death. 'We understood each other,' she said:

> He stayed in the military after the war, becoming deputy commander of the Urals Military District – I, and all our children, followed him around. He said, 'I am a pilot and a pilot must fly, a pilot cannot stay on the ground.' He encouraged me with what I needed to do, too; I did go to Moscow State University and became a professor of history – I have had a life of studying, writing, reading, lecturing and teaching – always living in Moscow, because I am a Moscovite.
>
> We have our big family too – three children, seven grand-children and fifteen great-grandchildren.
>
> My life has been a lesson; I have learned how to learn and I was always learning. I had a perfect school before the war, another unforgettable school during the war, and the 'everyday life school' where I am studying now.

The Soviet Union's victory and survival would, of course, have been an immense relief for those who came through; but for many of the young women – whilst not fearing death – the emotional pain of war continued, because in spite of what each woman might have achieved, serving alongside men on the front-line of war was, undoubtedly, an emotional rollercoaster for which they were not prepared – if indeed it is ever possible to prepare for such an experience. During their active years the women had had no option at all but to almost reject their feminity; as mentioned above, they had to wear their hair short, and they were also given men's uniforms to wear. They would, like the men, often have had to endure long days (sometimes weeks) at the front, without bathing or washing; indeed, in the course of my research, I read that what some of these women feared most of all was 'looking ugly at the time of death'.[8]

Also, whilst in combat, the different genders had to learn to work alongside each other, which was an unusual situation that did sometimes lead to conflict. Whilst there was no difference in the skills required for the task in hand – flying or sniping – the expectations could prove problematic, with the men often making the women's role still harder by expressing disapproval (even revulsion) about women behaving in a tough (or masculine) way, whilst still expecting them to perform as well as they did. However, to quote night bomber regiment pilot Nadezhda Popova again, comfort could be drawn too from the two genders coming together in this way. She said:

I don't think you can separate men from women in this situation. War does not spare anyone; it doesn't distinguish between the sexes or the young from the old. Battle is a who-will-win situation. They were destroying us and we were destroying them. There was no choice involved. That is the logic of war; it is life or death, victory or be vanquished.[9]

Anna Kirilina, a mechanic–ammo technician in Galina's regiment, referred to the strong friendships that developed between men, and between women; friendships that were tested to the extreme because they all knew that at any moment they could be killed. She said:

Wartime is wartime, and war is not a labour for women. We didn't even feel what was happening because we were so physically overstrained. The war made us not friends, but relatives. It made us sisters, dear, dear creatures to each other … for the four years of war, we all went through and experienced so much that sometimes it seems impossible for a human creature to know it in her whole lifetime.[10]

However, as alluded to earlier, whilst victory – and survival – was an inevitable relief, the post-war years were a tough emotional struggle too for many of the women fighters because, largely, the expectation was that they would fairly quickly return to domestic life. They were discouraged from pursuing military careers in favour of the men, returning from their own service on the front line. The primary goal for Russia after the war was to rebuild the country and women were essential in the civilian workforce; they were simply no longer needed in the military, but they were needed in the homes and they were needed to be mothers. Irina Rakobolskaya, Chief of Staff of the night bomber regiment, summed up the difficulties for many of the women, saying:

> I think that during the war, when the fate of our country was being decided, the bringing of women into aviation was justified. But in peacetime a woman can only fly for sport … otherwise how can one combine a career with a family and with maternal happiness?[11]

However, frustrations aside, many of the women also suffered hugely because of the emotional and physical scars of the war they could not escape from. Some were stigmatised and made to feel 'dirty' because they had spent time on the front line with men; others were traumatised by the killings they had accomplished. For these reasons, and many others, few women have spoken openly of their experience. This is why it is so important that Galina Brok-Beltsova has given me her story for this book. She shines a light on the memory of the women who flew, sniped and served alongside her. Undoubtedly, had the courage of the 800,000 women who came forward to serve Soviet Russia in 1941 not prevailed, the outcome of the Patriotic War could have been very different. That courage – indeed, this labour force – couldn't have come at a more challenging and vital time in the history of the Soviet Union. By October 1941 Hitler's invasion had already resulted in devastation and the capture of millions of Russian soldiers.

The attempt to take Moscow was carefully planned by Germany; it was a key part of their strategy to occupy as much of the country as they could during 'Operation Barbarossa' – which had begun four months earlier, in June. Hitler's confidence was possibly riding high at the beginning of the Battle of Moscow because Germany and Axis troops had, by this time, seized all the land up to and around Leningrad to the north and Ukraine to the south. The occupation of both these places proved to be equally brutal and hideous; it was Hitler's 'success' in Leningrad (now St Petersburg) that led to the 900-day siege of the city, during which over a million people died – 90 per cent of them through starvation. In Ukraine it was the Jews who fared the worst: between the Nazi's arrival in Autumn 1941 and mid-1944, over 1.5 million Ukrainian Jews were killed and a further 800,000 displaced.[12]

So determined was Germany to win over its rival of many years that for the purposes of Barbarossa about 80 per cent of the whole of the Wehrmacht (the German armed forces) were deployed in the Soviet Union. However, Moscow – for the Germans – did not prove to be another Leningrad or Ukraine. Hitler's army was – over several weeks – stalled and pushed back by the Soviet troops, who had strengthened the defence of their capital by recruiting over 1 million more troops, many of whom served in 1,000 new tanks. The weather, too, played its part – the muddy roads (*Rasputitsa* in Russian) on the outskirts of the capital made it harder than it would otherwise have been for the Germans to penetrate, and by the end of November temperatures were already dropping to around –20°C, and by December to a record low of –42°C, which grounded the Luftwaffe. In addition to strengthening the military (most of the extra recruits arriving from Siberia and the east following orders from Stalin), the Russians also outwitted their invaders by doing such things as disguising their roads – they turned their main streets into unrecognisable tracks and painted artificial roads over park-

ways and wastelands. Fake buildings were erected in the city, and the cleverest of all disguises were presented upon the Kremlin: the roofs of its palaces and cathedrals were painted a rusty brown so as to blend in with the houses around its walls, and its gardens were painted to look like campsites. It was a cunning, masterful tactic – one that worked.

Operation Barbarossa was the largest military operation in history, involving more men, tanks, guns and aircraft than in any other. However, whilst Hitler's failure to take Moscow made him resolve to rebuild and strengthen the Wehrmacht for two further offensives, what he did not count upon was the confidence it had given Stalin, with the Red Army, to fight until the end. Barbarossa was followed by

Galina Brok–Beltsova, *c.* 2020.

further occupation attempts in 1942 and 1943, culminating in the Battle of Stalingrad. Each time the Germans met with failure; but nevertheless victory for the Soviet Union came at a terrible cost. It is estimated that about 1,700 Soviet towns and a further 70,000 villages were brought to their knees.

Galina's figure of 27 million of her fellow Russians dying during the Great Patriotic War is possibly debatable – hopefully slightly lower, not higher – but still it is certain that the Soviet Union, in spite of ultimate victory, suffered dreadfully; and it is especially for those who died that Galina's story is told.

Finally, Galina asked me to end her story with a message she feels is particularly important. A lover of literature, Galina quoted a line from a famous Russian poem by Alexander Blok called 'The Twelve'. The line, she said, is: 'Keep a Revolutionary Step! The Restless Enemy will not stop.'

'Quite simply,' Galina Brok-Beltsova urged, 'we should all look to the future, carefully and diligently, and optimistically, always looking out for other people and thinking about how to develop and fortify our homeland.'

NOTES

1 www.airforcemag.com/article/not-just-night-witches/
2 the-past.com/feature/operation-bagration/
3 www.airvectors.net/avpe2.html
4 airpowerasia.com/2020/09/30/night-witches-the-all-female-soviet-night-bomber-aviators-of-ww-ii/
5 Amy Goodpaster Strebe, *Flying For Her Country: The American and Soviet Women Military Pilots of World War II*, Potomac Books Inc, 2009
6 www.nationalww2museum.org/war/articles/lady-death-red-army-lyudmila-pavlichenko
7 www.smithsonianmag.com/history/eleanor-roosevelt-and-the-soviet-sniper
8 Svetlana Alexeivich, *The Unwomanly Face of War*, Penguin Classics, 2017
9 Shelley Saywell, *Women in War*, Penguin, 1986
10 Anne Noggle, *A Dance with Death: Soviet Airwomen in World War II*, Texas AM University Press, 2002
11 Strebe, *Flying For Her Country*
12 www.britannica.com/place/Ukraine/The-Nazi-occupation-of-Soviet-Ukraine

ANKA ALUJEVIC: 'BUGS AND BUTTONS', A PARTISAN MEMORY FROM YUGOSLAVIA

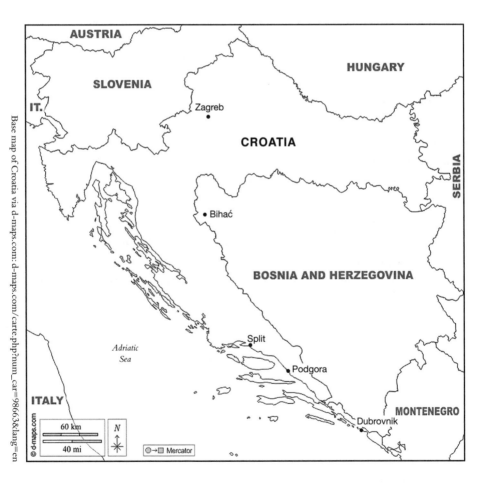

Base map of Croatia via d-maps.com: d-maps.com/carte.php?num_car=98663&lang=en

21 August 1943

My dear mother!

I have heard news today that those 'devils' are looking for Ante, and Divna. It is scary for me to hear this – but I am somewhat calmed by believing Ante has gone to Split, and I think is with Dad; and Divna is hiding not far from Podgora – where I think she will be safe.

And last week mother I saw Krasna, who was holding a machine-gun. We talked about everything for so long, she is very brave and bold, a real fighter! I have heard from comrades since I saw her that she is going to join the 'Commune District Committee'; but I hope she will have a little break from the fighting first and recover for a little while. I am on the committee now, as a secretary. Since I have been here, I haven't moved around very much, and it isn't too dangerous. As for the food mother, I am always full, and I have even gained a little more weight. I have as much bread as I want, and figs, grapes, carob and more.

But I do miss soap, I haven't been able to wash now for over ten days, I have written to someone in the next village to send some to me but haven't got any yet. Anyway mother, I can't help it I am always thinking about the traitors in Podgora; I am so frightened something will happen to you, please try to keep yourself safe. I would be so pleased if you could come and see us in the mountains. If Mirna has not yet gone to Split to be with Dad, please don't let her go. You can see that new events are happening every day. Take care of her too, I know you will, and Olja. I hear Lili has joined an acting group and is performing, that is nice.

My wound, mother, I am afraid has got worse; I think it is infected, so if you can – in addition to soap – please send me pieces of cloth (which you must first boil), and some antiseptic, and bandages.

And mother watch out, please, as to who you talk to and be careful with what you say. Avoid provocation and strange questions. Anyone could be a Ustasha, without you knowing. I dream of being in Split with my father. Beware mother, I know this is such a hard time, but we have to fight. One day it will be another world, our world in which we will both have joy.

When you write to me, write to me about everything; about you, about all my sisters, our friends in Podgora – tell me how they are. Tell me too about the 'devils' but mention no names.

Many greetings to all mother, you are loved and greeted by your
Anka

'Death to Fascism, Freedom to the People'.

Anka (then Anka Nola) was 19 years old when she wrote this letter, in August 1943, whilst she was in 'in the woods' with the Partisan resistance, in mountains near her native town of Podgora, in the south of Croatia. She was the second eldest of seven children – six girls and one boy, who was the second youngest. By this time the Second World War in Croatia had caused her family to become separated, as the letter explains. The recollection of her own physical pain runs parallel with the constant anxiety she lived with about the safety and well-being of all her siblings and her parents. As this letter was written, Croatia was under occupation by the Italians – just a few weeks later that occupation would cease with their capitulation – but the war by that time had already wreaked havoc, death, and misery. The passage of time can never be turned back. Anka's life – indeed everyone's – had changed for always.

Anka (centre) with sisters Divna (left) and Lili, c. 1941.

Anka was 17 when the war was announced in Croatia in the spring of 1941 – an intelligent child becoming a young woman in a home she described as 'disciplined' but blessed, with loving parents who brought up their children calmly and peacefully, surrounding them with books and music. She refers to all her siblings in this letter: Krasna, born in 1923 – a year before Anka; Lili, who was born two years after Anka, in 1926, followed by the arrival of Divna in 1928, Mirna in 1930, Ante (the only boy) in 1932 and Olja in 1933. The closeness of her family inevitably would have made the pain of separation harder; but perhaps it strengthened her too – even in the darkest moments of war those who know of happiness at least can hope of that again in the future.

In the summer of 1943, when this letter was written, the Second World War in Croatia had been under way for well over two years; intensifying by the day with the Partisan Resistance continuing in its determination to drive out the Fascists who had occupied the country since it became aligned with Germany, and Italy, in April 1941. However, even before Axis alignment was confirmed and Croatia became an 'independent state' in the spring of 1941, its Prime Minister, Ante Pavelić, had been moving the country in an increasingly nationalistic direction. Prior to that time he had established an organisation called the Ustaše, which he ran within Croatia, enabling him to pursue his (and the Axis's) fascist objectives. From then onwards, until the Italians capitulated two and half years later, Croatia existed as a 'puppet' state of Germany and Italy, 'independent' in name only; to all intents and purposes it was entirely dependent on them and obliged to follow their orders.

And Pavelić, together with the Ustaše, certainly did follow orders – between 1941 and the end of the war he oversaw the persecution of many racial minorities and political opponents in Croatia, including Serbs, Jews, Romani, and other anti-fascists, and was directly instrumental in the killing of many Jews in the Holocaust in Croatia. Some 300,000 Croatians were murdered by the Ustaše alone during the war. Pavelić, above all, wanted to eliminate Croatia's Serb minority, through a process of expulsion and extermination.[1]

Pockets of resistance sprang up in Croatia almost immediately in response to the position taken by Pavelić, initially comprised of Croatia's Serbs, but it was the Partisans who provided the resistance with leadership and a clear programme, under Marshal Josip Broz Tito. It was also the Partisans who stepped forward to courageously demonstrate – in considerable numbers – that the savage practices of the Ustaše would not be tolerated. Anka remembers well the moment, in April 1941, that she was told of her country's allegiance with the German Axis, even though this was over eighty years ago. She said:

> I was studying at the Trade Academy in Split at the time. I loved my school, and I greatly respected our headmaster. Then, suddenly, one day he came into class with an Italian man, who was a fascist. We studied Italian and German at the academy, and we understood completely when he interrupted our director, who always spoke to us in Croatian, and said: 'Speak Italian, this is no longer Croatia, this is Italy.' For the first time in my life I was offended. Offended and angry.
>
> At home, our parents were very scared. They read newspapers and listened to the radio. They knew of the evil of fascism because of what had happened in Poland. One afternoon they gathered us older children around and told us what could come upon us. I remember the sentence 'you will be hungry and dreaming of bread.' It was incomprehensible to me.
>
> Shortly after that Split, where were living, was bombed. The Yugoslav kingdom disappeared after Italian troops entered – fascist terror had started.

Up to that point, Anka described the joy of her childhood; her father had worked in New Zealand for twenty years in the rubber industry, achieving prosperity which enabled him to provide generously for his family. She lived in Podgora during her early years, in a home surrounded by olive trees and vineyards. However, when she was about 10 years old the family moved to Split, because the schools were better – but kept their home in Podgora. Of her childhood she said:

> It was disciplined, but filled with love, care, attention and harmony. Everything was planned 'by the hour' – when we ate, when we studied, when we played – and we all had a small task in the house, too. At 9 p.m. we had to be in bed and were allowed to read until 10 p.m., and after that our parents would check us all to make sure lights were off. We read a lot; our mother was obsessed with books.

Music and dancing were important to Anka from an early age; indeed, appreciation of the arts was strongly encouraged by both her parents. Anka said her family was the first in Podgora to get a radio and a record player; and she told of how she used to sing with her mother in the village choir and that her family would sing together, whilst her father played a small guitar. Anka's love and appreciation of music, instilled by her parents, has stayed with her whole life, giving her comfort and joy, including during the war years, which you will read of a little later. Anka said, 'When the world is quiet, there is nothing more beautiful than a good book and classical music, they fill me with peace, and calm me down.'

However, inevitably, as it did for everyone, everything changed with the announcement of war: peace, provision of everyday essentials, togetherness and security disappeared; no-one could any more take for granted the life for which they had previously felt blessed.

Not long after Split was taken by the Italians in April 1941, Anka and her family moved back to their home in Podgora, hoping and believing it would be safer than Split. It was safer, to some extent, but not entirely. Anka spoke of Podgora, too, being raided by the Ustaše and Italians from time to time, and about torpedoes that attacked their ships in the Adriatic Sea (which runs along the Croatian coast). She said that by January the following year Podgora was half-occupied. The family did not join the Partisan movement immediately, but shortly after their return there from Split they were contacted by anti-fascist activists, in part because of their membership of the Croatian Peasant Party (known as the HSS), which represented mostly farmers and the poorer members of society. Very soon the whole family did join the resistance, Anka's elder sister, Krasna, being the first to 'take up a rifle', as a member of the First Proletarian Brigade – quite something for a girl of just 18 years. This brigade, established by Josip Broz Tito, was one of the 'elite' formations within the Partisan movement, also part of the National Liberation Army of Yugoslavia.

Krasna's departure 'into the woods', which is how Anka refers to actively supporting the Partisan cause, marked the beginning of her family becoming divided because of the war. The youngest children – Mirna, Ante, and Olja – were taken by their father to Split, without their mother; Divna, the fourth eldest of the sisters went into hiding in a village south of Podgora, and Lili, the third daughter, served the Partisans, first in the 'free' town of Livno in Bosnia, looking after them in her capacity as a singer and performer – skills desired amongst the troop leaders who respected the importance of leisure as a way of rebuilding strength. However, Lili died later on in the war, killed during the 'Fifth Offensive' – a fight also known as the Battle of Sutjeska because it took place in Bosnia near the river of the same name. This battle marked a key turning point in the history of the war in Yugoslavia, because it was the final major joint German–Italian operation against the Partisans. Even though many more Partisans (including Lili) were killed than Axis troops, the Fascists could not claim a decisive victory because the Partisan movement was quickly able to replenish troop numbers afterwards.[2] Anka was very proud of her sister, but the news of her death was – she said – the saddest day of all for her during the whole of the war, possibly the whole of her life. Of Lili, she said:

> Lili was 17 years old when she joined the Partisans … She was the most beautiful of all six sisters in our family, if we only talk about appearance. She was also the smartest of us all; she went with the actors to Livno, where she was able to perform. But the Fifth Offensive followed, and a mass retreat of Partisans and people towards Sutjeska began, where all trace of her was lost in the chaos. We never found out where Lili was, or how she died, or where her grave is. A friend told me he had to tell me the sad news.
>
> In that mayhem, my sister took care of some children who were refugees, children without fathers or mothers. She was also seen as kind and 'gifted' to be able to care like this by her some of her classmates, who would have been with her at the time. With these children, she (allegedly) took refuge in an improvised hospital, in a barracks where they were picked up by Chetniks[3] and set on fire alive.

Anka recalled then, again, her love of music; and the song that gave her 'small comfort' during this time of extreme grief. She said:

> It was the time of the song, such were the times; I loved to sing most, and most of all the 'Konjuh planinom' (Horse on the Mountain) arrangement by Oscar Danon[4] is my favourite – whom I was lucky to meet later, whilst in exile in Italy. When I heard about Lili's death, at the urging of a comrade, I sang it out loud without tears, then a mother of one of the children came who did not know our Lili was dead.

Anka, herself, served the Partisans within its 'agitprop' unit[5], using her secretarial and writing skills to spread the message of anti-fascism as widely as she could. She started this work at the beginning of 1942, as a youth leader visiting villages in the Dalmatia area of southern Croatia, near the coast, and in the mountainous region of Biokovo.

Anka's reference to 'agitprop' struck me; it is important because of the reminder it gives us that conflict is as much an emotional battle as it is physical. The way we decide to behave is often, inevitably, very much out of our control – but not always. Often, we are led by hearts and minds; our thoughts driven by the persuasiveness of others. 'Agitprop' is a shortened term for 'agitation and propaganda'; therefore Anka's work as a determined, confirmed communist persuading others to join the Partisan cause was vital; as essential as those carrying rifles or other weapons, because the Fascists were proving themselves to be not only strong, but well organised – and terrifyingly successful with the numbers of men, women and children they killed, imprisoned, left displaced or fearfully injured in Croatia – indeed throughout Yugoslavia and (of course) in many other parts of the world.

The term 'agitprop' actually has its roots in Russia, established – formally – in the communist party led by Vladimir Lenin in the 1900s. Many units within the communist party in the (then) Soviet Union had an 'agitation and propaganda' section, communist party 'agitators' being the chief points of contact between the party and the public.

However, Josip Broz Tito – the leader and driver of the Partisan movement in Yugoslavia during the Second World War – was certainly no 'puppet' of Russia, despite sharing the communist ideals of Lenin and Stalin. After leading the Yugoslav partisan movement during the war, Tito became the leader of the Socialist Federal Republic of Yugoslavia in 1953, leading until his death in 1980. During these post-war years, whilst in office, he pursued economic and foreign policy objectives that did not align with the interests of the Soviet Union and its Eastern Bloc allies, thus establishing himself as something of an 'independent' Communist leader. Not only after the war, but during the war as leader of the Partisan resistant movement, Tito was a leader who was able to not only develop a clear vision of what he considered essential for his beloved Yugoslavia but follow it through.

Brigadier Sir Fitzroy Maclean was a Scottish writer, soldier, and politician who spent some of the Second World War fighting in the Western desert campaign, specialising in commando raids, and on the ground in Yugoslavia, during which time he came to know Tito – whilst they were both immersed amongst the partisans. Of Tito, he wrote:

> There were many unexpected things about him; his surprisingly broad out-look; his never-failing sense of humour; his unashamed delight in the minor pleasures of life, a natural diffidence in human relationships giving way to a natural friendliness; a violent temper, flaring sudden rages; a considerateness and a generosity; and a surprising readiness to see two sides of a question. These were human qualities, hard to reconcile with the usual conception of a Communist puppet which made possible a better personal relationship between us that I had dared hope for.[6]

Anka was proud, and surprised, to be selected to attend an important meeting of the Partisan hierarchy, in December 1942 – this meeting was the 'First Congress of the Anti-Fascist Youth of Yugoslavia', in the city of Bihać, in the north-west of Bosnia. It was a strategically placed meeting because a month earlier the Partisans had successfully liberated the city from Nazi occupation during a two-week battle resulting in a clear and decisive victory – following which Bihać became the headquarters for the whole of the Yugoslavian Partisan movement.[7]

Tito was amongst those present at the Congress. Of meeting him, Anka recalled he 'seemed as striking as a film actor; funny, eloquent, open and not at all official.' She also remembered being impressed with many of the high-profile partisan leaders she met at this gathering, including Ivo Lola Ribar, whom she described as Yugoslavia's Che Guevara. I should just remind you that at the time of this meeting Anka was only 18 years old – it must have been quite something for her to be in the presence of such seniority; Tito was the most senior, but closely followed by Lola (as she refers to him), who was in charge of the Young Communist League of Yugoslavia during the war. Indeed, Anka recalled a lively and quite exquisite memory of time spent with Lola, saying:

> We had finished a dinner, after which there was dancing. Lola approached me and asked me why I wasn't dancing; and would I dance? I said yes, and after that we danced two normal dances, then some waltzes and a tango, I don't

remember exactly, we also danced to some chansons. And as we danced, we talked about everything, not just fighting and war; we talked about culture, about many things. He asked me what 'attracted' me to the partisan cause, and we talked about both of our families …

However, Lola was killed whilst fighting for the Partisans in 1943, as was his brother Jurica. His mother was executed by Germans in 1944, leaving only his father Ivan who, in spite of his grief (but possibly driven by it), went onto become head of state in Yugoslavia, serving in this role until 1953 when Marshal Tito was elected to the new post of President of the Republic. Lola was later posthumously proclaimed a National Hero of Yugoslavia – one of around 1,300 people to receive this accolade.

The fact she was invited to this meeting reflects her own seniority within the Yugoslav Partisan movement, how good she was at spreading the vital anti-fascism message, and also (I am sure) how well thought of she was. However, mixing in the 'higher echelons' of the Partisan movement did not protect her from the ugly reality of war. Some memories have stayed with her, all these years, dispelling any doubts at all that – quite simply – everything about war is horrific. She said:

War is first of all chaos, suffering, death. There is everything in war. I remember the public shooting of an Ustasha who was sentenced to death by the People's Court. Somewhere in Ravča, in the vicinity of Vrgorac (in Croatia), it happened, there was shooting day and night. I do not remember the name or rank of that one captured Ustasha, who was to be shot for the crimes he committed. He was a young man; his hands were tied behind his back when he was shot. The Ustasha had small legs; 'take off his boots, it's your number' the poor fellow in the firing squad told me, but I couldn't do it. 'What you can't do, I do' he replied, and lifted one of the man's legs, and I saw him jerk. I was shocked. Comrades joked at my expense because I was hypersensitive. It was only then I realised what war was. Everyone's death is hard for me, no matter who it is.

Before that, I was occasionally in combat and 'sticking' on the ground to some company, I once dragged a wounded comrade in blood, and I was out of breath when I first saw death, a dead man up close. I was horrified, it hit me hard, it's not 'just like that' – to kill a man.

The 'occasional combat' role Anka is referring to above is some fighting she took part in for a short while after Italy capitulated in September 1943, in the Vrgorac region, in the far south of Croatia. It was here, she said, that she encountered many badly wounded Partisans for the first time. However, she was unable to fight for long because it was during that autumn that Anka became dangerously ill with a typhoid infection that almost killed her.

She was transferred, together with many other Croatians also wounded, sick, and weakened by war, to the island of Hvar, not far off Croatia's Dalmatian coast, where there was a hospital. Shortly before she was due to be moved to another island – Vis, which lies further from the coast in the Adriatic Sea – Anka recorded the frustration, despair, and sheer pain she experienced whilst being ill with the following words, written at Christmas in 1943:

It is a month since I have been lying in bed with typhus. Lying down for a long time brings me to think and watch, everything. There is a moment, more than one, when I am so angry, because I see a mess around me, and more in my comrades. I don't see any life in these people. You could die over them and they are so ill they would not notice …

Tonight, it is clear and cold, there is a little bora blowing. In the course of the last two nights, we have become even more confused, I think we should leave urgently.

Her diary entry for 26 December 1943 states:

In Stari Grad (a coastal town in the north of Hvar) there was a great bustle of people. At midnight, the sick people in five ships were packed. I helped with the boarding, although I felt very weak, especially in my stomach. In great torment many were vomiting. It is terrible, there are storms at sea, huge rolling waves. We arrived at Vis in the morning – lots of people were singing, we looked across to Italy. It was one of the hardest moments I can remember, leaving my country, my family, my comrades …

Anka spent a few days on the island of Vis, still sick, but also busy help-ing many other refugees and evacuees. Vis has its own – quite remarkable – Second World War story; after Italian capitulation almost all the islands around Yugoslavia's coast were occupied by the Nazis, with the exception of Vis. It became, therefore, a refuge for many Croatians, who went there quite simply because they wanted to be safe. However, even though it is small (only 8km north to south and 17km east to west) it took on a vital role during the war not only for the refugees but for the Partisans – at one point it was the (secret) location of Tito's headquarters – and it also housed an RAF airfield, used by Hawker Hurricane squadrons and Spitfire pilots flying in support of ground troops fighting in Italy.

However, Anka's short time on Vis at the end of 1943 and beginning of 1944 was far from happy; she was there on her way to Italy, deeply troubled that she had had to leave Croatia behind and not knowing when (or possibly even if) she would return. Her diary entry for 3 January 1944 states:

> I can't write about my feelings the moment. I have had to leave my country, my homeland. It shines before my eyes with tears, but it's all for nothing, and bitterness, and tears, everything. It must go. Oh, how terrible it is …
>
> We're travelling in two English warships, Destroyers. There is a terrible and desperate storm. I was assigned to the bow, where the waves and the sea constantly blow over us. It hurts, I am so wet and cold. Everything is vain, but one must stand firm and suffer together with all the suffering people …

Eventually, after her arrival in southern Italy by boat and lorry, Anka's health began to improve and she was given a job, with the Partisans, as chairman of the Central Youth Committee. She was responsible for the care of Croatian refugee children who had gone to Italy, many of whom had lost their parents in the war. This role gave her a chance to travel to many different towns and villages; she said:

> Santa Maria de Cesarea, Santa Maria de Bagno, Santa Maria di Nardo – these are just some of the places I stayed. I was separated from my family in the chaos of war, and these children became my family. I organised their schooling, I did all I could to take care of them. Some of them contacted me after the war and thanked me; and I would ask them if they knew anything about their parents, which was usually not the case.[8]

This was a very busy time for Anka, and a joyous one too because it was whilst she was here that she was reunited with her father, brother, and two youngest sisters. Their mother, by this time leader of the group 'Anti-Fascist Women of Dalmatia', arrived soon afterwards. The reunion, first with her father, was entirely fortuitous – it happened whilst Anka was being 'wooed' by a British soldier. This is how she put it:

> One of the young officers often came to see me as he liked me a lot. But there was a language barrier between us. I knew some German and Italian, but he didn't. He told me he had a good interpreter so one day he brought him to me – and he was my father! My God, this was such happiness. Especially when I heard that Mirna, Olja and Ante were with him. At that time, I didn't know where any of my family were … after that I didn't have much time for the young officer, but he was a gentleman to the end. He brought me chocolate all the time, and for the first time I had chewing gum …

This was not the only British troop memory Anka recalled from during her time in Italy. It makes me wonder how often she got the better of these young men … I hope they enjoyed this moment as much as she did. She recalled, with amusement, what happened after she arrived in Santa Maria de Leuca, in the very far south of Italy:

> After a while, we were introduced to some of the Allies, mostly the English. At first, we were greeted quite coldly and restrainedly – just like real Englishmen (ha, huh). Namely, they saw us as some communists, Bolsheviks. They were quite cautious and mean to us. That's when I suggested to my friends that we host an event in one of the great halls. There were a lot of soldiers, but also officers. I was the first to perform with a song my dad taught me when I was a kid, aged about 6. I sang it in English. I think it was called 'Its long way…', it was more like a bright military march. [Perhaps it was 'It's a long way to Tipperary?] After the end, thunderous applause broke through the hall, rapturous shouts of approval. The English were thrilled. By God, they didn't expect it from some peasant back in the Balkans! Afterwards we performed many more of our songs of fighting, but also popular songs, and we danced. The English literally went mad with elation. That's how we broke the cold English ice. Later, everything was easier with communication. There were packages of clothes, medicine, food. My best was tea biscuits, but also chocolate bars. Yes, after that event, I received from an officer as a gift, an almost a new

upper part of their uniform with a Yugoslav flag, which tightened at the waist. It looked perfect on me. I was so proud!

★★★

Whilst war takes so much away, it also gives; and it was during the Second World War that Anka met her husband, Zarko Alujević. She met him first at the meeting in Bihać, in 1942, referred to earlier in this chapter. She spoke about her exhaustion when she arrived at this meeting, because her journey – from southern Croatia – had taken almost three weeks, by truck travelling over mountains in snowy, blizzarding conditions. Upon her arrival she recalled being welcomed into a small, but warm hut, and the first person she noticed was a presentable, thin man in the elegant uniform of a captain. The man was Zarko. In her words:

> He took off his jacket and, even though he seemed so elegant, began to pull bugs off his clothes, his skin and his hair; and he counted them as he threw them into the fire. When he got to number ninety-nine I told him I was sick of the counting, to which he said, 'If miss has had enough, please to help me get rid of the rest as quickly as possible.' And so, together, with the crackle of fire, we cleared him of the bugs and lice. This was our first meeting …

Later that same day, at the conference, they danced together, but after two days they were separated; Zarko returned to the battlefield and Anka to her propaganda work. They didn't meet again until the autumn of 1944, where they were reunited at another Partisan gathering, this time in Anka's home-town of Split. This time, there were no 'bugs', but 'buttons'; Anka said she spotted him at the far side of a crowded room, struggling with a broken button on his jacket, so she approached him and offered to mend it. He agreed she could, but wouldn't remove the jacket, so she had to stand close to him …

Zarko and Anka married at the end of 1945, in Split. They were together for fifty-six years, until his death in 2001. They have two sons, Ognjen and Ranko, born in 1948 and 1951, four grandchildren and a great-grandson.

After the war, Zarko became an eminent ship-building engineer, specialising in the construction of warships and submarines. He was highly

Anka and Zarko after their wedding in Split, end of 1945.

Anka with Zarko and their family, 1931.

respected in the military, too, advancing to the rank of lieutenant general in the army. Anka was justifiably proud of him, and recalled, too, his friendship with Randolph Churchill (son of Winston Churchill), whom he met on the island of Vis. She said:

> Mr Churchill gave my husband some chocolate, which was an incredible luxury during the war, and they became friends. My husband used to say that Randolf Churchill, a member of the British elite, simply adored our movement and our people!

Finally, I would like to end Anka's Second World War memory with a return to her love of reading, and writing. Her son Ranko, who has provided me with his mother's precious story so I can tell you about the remarkable fortitude of Partisan women in Yugoslavia during the war, also told me his mother loves to write poetry, and prose. She wrote the following words whilst she was in Italy in 1944, feeling alone and homesick for Croatia:

> There is a quiet wind blowing from the north. I sit and listen to the murmur of the sea, and through each of its showers, I hear words coming to me from a

Anka, 2020.

distance. It seems that this murmuring is whispering to me about the One who is so far from us, but which is somehow still close to our hearts. It is as if that quiet wind from the north, and the waves coming from a distance, really speak of the One, our dearest, which is far from us, about the One that we would so gladly see and live in - our Homeland.

A Historical Note

Throughout the war years, under Marshal Tito, support for the Partisans continued to expand; by the middle of 1944 most of Croatia, apart from some of the main cities, had been liberated. Many of those who had served with the Ustaša fled (including Pavelić) – in fear of Partisan reprisal – towards Allied troops further north; but the British commanders refused to accept their surrender and handed them over to the Partisans, who, in turn, sent many to death camps.

Around six months after the end of the Second World War, Yugoslavia became the Federal People's Republic until 1963, when it was declared the Socialist Federal Republic (of Yugoslavia.) In 2006, after a series of conflicts and bitter infighting within the Republic the union was finally disbanded.

Ante Pavelić died in Austria in 1959.

NOTES

1 ushmm.org/content/en/article/jasenovac
2 Phyllis Auty, 'Yugoslavia, September 1943/May 1945' in *Purnell's History of the Second World War*, Vol. 4, Phoebus Publishing Ltd, c. 1970
3 www.britannica.com/topic/Chetnik
4 www.youtube.com/watch?v=FSf26kBPA2E (see p. 170 for a translation)
5 www.britannica.com/topic/agitprop
6 Sir Fitzroy Maclean, 'The Work of the Resistance, 1939/45' in *Purnell's History of the Second World War*, Vol. 7, Phoebus Publishing Ltd, c. 1970
7 www.jutarnji.hr
8 Ibid.

Translation of 'Konjuh planinom': 'Horse on the Mountain'

Horse on the mountain, the wind rustles, hums,
leaves sing mournful songs …
Pines and firs, maples and birches
they curl up next to each other …
The night shrouded the whole forest in black,
Konjuh moans, rocks fall …
A dead friend, a crying miner
buried by a partisan company …
Autumn rains fell on the grave,
barrels of snow bones blew up …
And on top of the mountain the flag is flying,
red of proletarian blood …

EPILOGUE

FIONA SYMON: A REMEMBRANCE STORY ABOUT THE SINKING OF THE *LANCASTRIA* IN JUNE 1940

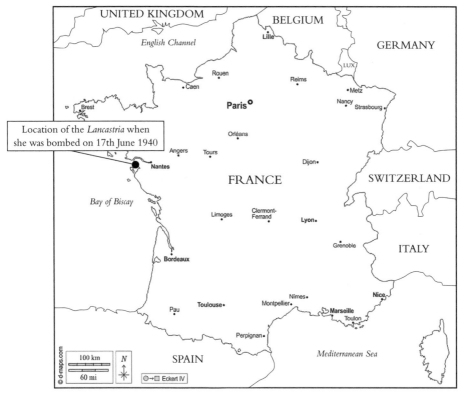

Location of the *Lancastria* when she was bombed on 17th June 1940

Base map of France via d-maps.com: d-maps.com/carte.php?num_car=18005&lang=en

I have chosen to present Fiona's Second World War story as an epilogue because it differs from the other chapters in this book; it does not, as the others do, tell of her own experience of the war; rather it tells of how she has been affected, and to some extent defined, by one single wartime event that has had devastating consequences not only for her but for thousands of others. As will shortly be revealed, this epilogue refers to one of the Second World War's darkest and best-kept secrets – which is less of a secret today thanks to the determination of Fiona that the thousands who died and were hurt that day should – and will – be remembered.

Fiona's story is as much about the tragedy that left her without her father, Andrew Richardson, as it is about her lifelong campaign for Remembrance. Through her grief and determination for recognition she has brought comfort to hundreds of others – and relentlessly championed the cause of openness, no matter how exhausting it has sometimes been for her to continue along this journey.

★★★

Fiona Symon was just 10 months old on 17 June 1940, at home with her mother in Fife the day the British troopship *Lancastria* was struck by four German bombs whilst she was anchored near the mouth of the River Loire, in the Charpentier roads, close to St Nazaire in the west of France. *Lancastria's* departure was imminent: some 6,000 passengers had already boarded – mostly British troops and Royal Air Force personnel, but also French and Belgian refugees seeking escape from their countries' occupation by German troops.

The precise number of those who perished that day will never be known, as accurate records of those who had boarded did not exist, but it is known that Rudolph Sharp, *Lancastria's* captain, was instructed to take up to 9,000 men, women and children; only around 2,500 were confirmed afterwards as surviving. *Lancastria* keeled over almost immediately after the bombs hit the deck at around 4 p.m. that day, sinking her in less than half an hour. Many of those who weren't killed immediately were machine-gunned whilst trying to swim to safety or were on board one of the many small lifeboats that would otherwise have taken them to shore.

The sinking of *Lancastria* was then, and remains, the worst ever maritime disaster in Britain's history. It represents the largest loss of life for British forces in the whole of the Second World War. But still, over eighty years later (as this is written), despite the vast scale of the catastrophe, the sinking of *Lancastria* remains largely unknown. It is little spoken of except by those who grieve, and her broken hull is a corroding wreck in the cold water of the Atlantic Ocean that has not been given war grave status under British law. The lack of 'official' recognition over the years has exacerbated the sadness of those who lost loved ones, not least of all because it has meant that many questions about how, and why, the tragedy occurred have remained unanswered, creating confusion and a feeling for those left behind that their loved ones died in vain. *Lancastria* was designed to hold 2,200 passengers – why, then, did the captain overload her to such an extent, and who was giving him orders to do so? Why didn't she leave her anchorage as soon as she was full? A better understanding for the relatives would at least provide them with some sort of closure.

The 'secrecy' was intentional at the beginning. Prime Minister Winston Churchill issued a 'D' notice as soon as he was told about it, prohibiting publicity of the story.[1] The instruction for silence at the time can probably be explained by the timing of the disaster: France had all but fallen into German occupation by 17 June 1940; it capitulated the following day. Belgium, the Netherlands and Luxembourg had fallen six weeks earlier. Morale amongst British troops, who had fought with the Allies to prevent the occupation, was low – which Churchill would have been extremely conscious of. It was a dire situation with the threat of an invasion of Britain looming.

Several years after the war ended, Churchill recalled his decision to prohibit news of the sinking of *Lancastria*, saying that at the time it was because there was already so much happening that was disastrous. He said he hadn't intended to forget about it completely, but he was taken over by events.

Churchill's 'D' notice, referred to above, is still in place, and is not due to expire until 2040 (at the time of it being issued in 1940 it was given with a 100-year timeline). The revelations that may or may not come out in nineteen years (from the date this is written) will be of little purpose so long after the hurt occurred.

If this book achieves anything in addition to better understanding about the experience of women during the Second World War, it will lead people to talk about failures of leadership that led to loss of life such as that on the *Lancastria*; ideally her demise will one day be as widely known as other equally tragic sinkings, such as the *Titanic* in 1912 and the *Lusitania* in 1915. Fiona does have peace of mind that she – with the help of many, whose names are listed at the end of this chapter – has done all she can for those who died and those who mourn, but it still saddens her that there may still be hidden secrets. She is also disappointed that the decision has been taken not to grant the wreck of *Lancastria* protection under British law. The British government's reason for not taking this latter action is because the wreck is in French territorial waters and the 1986 Protection of Military Remains Act does not give Britain jurisdiction to give a shipwreck not in our own water this status, also arguing that the 'French government has provided an appropriate level of protection to *Lancastria* through French law, which does gives the wreck the formal status and protection it deserves'.

The French have, to be fair, done much to honour those who died: there is protection around *Lanastria*'s sunken hull preventing divers from swimming down to her, there is a memorial in St Nazaire and many graves have been created for those (including Fiona's father) whose bodies washed up on their shore. But this is not enough for Fiona and the many British relatives who would still like the British government to do more, because – after all – they were British troops, not French. Fiona's father, who was a journalist by trade but during the war served as a private in the Royal Army Service Corps, was one of around 150,000 British troops left behind in France following the Dunkirk evacuation. She said:

> My father's body was found five weeks after *Lancastria* sank; he is buried in the seaside village of Beauvoir-sur-Mer. But my mother didn't get confirmation of his death for three years. If Churchill hadn't forgotten to lift the ban he would have saved the families a lot of heartache. My mother never recovered. Even after the war was finished, I remember finding her staring at the road to the station. When I reminded her he was dead she said that some of them were taken prisoner and, you never know, he might come back. My mother had the words, 'Still, still with thee when purple morning breaketh' inscribed on his gravestone.

★★★

Fiona Symon has been at the forefront of campaigning for recognition of *Lancastria* for many years; deeply empathetic for those who lost so much, as she did, but also instinctively driven to the cause out of love and respect for her father, instilled within her as she grew up by those around her who knew him. She said:

> My father was well known in Kirkcaldy, where we lived; people told me how he always had a smile on his face, and always made people feel special. His career was journalism, but he was also organist and choirmaster at Whtyscauseway Baptist Church, where his father (my grandfather) had been the minister. When he went into the army he wasn't in a fighting unit, apparently this was because he knew he would never have been able to kill anyone. Through the years many people who knew him spoke to me about him, but my mother couldn't talk about him. I suppose that was the same for many families.
>
> It is said that you never miss what you never had, but in my mind that isn't true. All my life I have missed the presence of a father. As a small child it was a puzzled feeling of being somehow different – the only child in my class without this person called a father, and as a teenager I was sad and angry at missing out on the relationship my friends enjoyed.
>
> But I gradually came to terms with a situation I couldn't change. I married, brought up my son Andrew, named after my father, and had a daughter – Jill. I put *Lancastria* out of my mind as I had become convinced I would never learn anymore.

However, in May 2005 Fiona came to the realisation that she hadn't, and couldn't, put *Lancastria* out of her mind. After attending a talk by author Jonathan Fenby, who wrote a book about the tragedy, she came across others who like her were still confused and grieving. She said:

> I realised then I needed to do something for the wonderful, talented and greatly loved man my father was – and also for those who died with him.
>
> Before he sailed to France in February 1940, my father wrote in his diary of how he had always tried to maintain honour and the bond of his pledged word. I wonder what he would think of his country's governments over the years since the tragedy. I do know that had he lived he would have been at the forefront of our fight for justice. Although the result has often been sleepless

nights, I am grateful for the opportunity I have had to work for justice for all of those involved in the tragedy.

I promised then to do everything I could to ensure that my father and the thousands who died with him on *Lancastria* are at last acknowledged, and remembered with honour, for all time, by the country they gave their lives for.

There began Fiona's tireless campaigning, for which she was awarded an MBE in the Queen's 2021 New Year's Honours list. She has, indeed, achieved admirable success with her campaigning; there is now a commemorative medal, simply called The *Lancastria* Medal, which was commissioned by the Scottish government and given to connected families in 2008.

Much of Fiona's campaigning has been done as chairman of the *Lancastria* Association of Scotland, since 2005. Through the association she has continued to bring relatives together, and over the years there have also been visits to St Nazaire to see the graves and attend the memorial stone located in the French harbour.

The most outstanding achievement of the *Lancastria* Association of Scotland[2] is the permanent memorial designed by Fife sculptor Marion Smith and unveiled in 2011. The memorial is a bronze sculpture representing the early steel construction of the ribs of *Lancastria* set on a granite block. It stands in the grounds of the Golden Jubilee National Hospital at Clydebank, on the land where she was built by William Beardmore and Son's shipyard, with commemorative text saying:

HMT *Lancastria*, sunk by enemy action 17th June 1940 at St Nazaire. The greatest loss of life in British maritime history. We will remember them.

In the foyer of the hospital there is a detailed model of *Lancastria*, painstakingly built over the course of a year by the late surgeon Mr Brian Dean, who presented it to the *Lancastria* Association of Scotland in 2013. At his request, the model was unveiled by Fiona as chair of the Association. Under the case are four storyboards telling the life of the ship. In a bookcase beside there is also a book of remembrance. The hospital, with its memorial, is a place of comfort for the families that has brought many relatives together for services on Remembrance Day and on the anniversary of the tragedy many times since it was unveiled in October 2013.

Fiona Symon MBE, with faithful friend Bruar, in 2020.

Her campaigning has also taken her to Downing Street; in 2007 she delivered a petition to then Prime Minister Tony Blair asking for what the families felt they needed most of all – that the British government designate the wreck of *Lancastria* an official war grave, by giving it full legal protection under British law, even though it lies in French waters. The petition had thousands of signatures, including those of Members of Parliament in England and Scotland, members of the Lords and senior figures in the armed forces. Upon delivering the petition Fiona said:

> There is a very real sense of anger amongst relatives that the lives of those who died and, indeed, the survivors who had to live with horrific memories, seem to be of less value than others who are remembered with honour. Those thousands of men who died, one of them my father, also gave their lives for their country.
>
> Triumphs in war are remembered and celebrated. Disasters are not. Yet the sheer magnitude of the loss of life when the *Lancastria* was sunk on the 17th of June 1940 cries out for acknowledgement by our government.

This book is, above all, a 'remembrance' book; it is a tribute to the women who lived through these years, written so that we can know more about the vital role they played in contributing to the peace we have had in the years that have followed. But for remembrance to be meaningful we have to have an understanding of what it is we are being asked to remember. That is why the revelations in this book are important – each of the chapters prior to this epilogue describe not only experiences, but what those experiences felt like, too. These revelations will, I hope, deepen understanding of these aspects of the Second World War, thus enabling longer lasting and more meaningful remembrance.

However, this epilogue takes us a step further. This is a history book; but Fiona Symon's story is not only about the past, it is about the present and the future – she has drawn our attention to a hugely significant event of the Second World War that still needs 'action' now for it to be correctly remembered and understood in the future. Fiona said:

> Right up until she died in 1992, my mother was still very sad and bitter that, come November when it's Armistice time, and the words 'lest we forget' are in every paper, mother used to say, 'yes and rightly so, but they've forgotten about the *Lancastria*.'

I am sad to read of the sadness of Daisy Richardson, Fiona's mother; that she didn't find peace after her husband died, and that she remained bitter. However, her daughter Fiona could not have done more to lift the memory of the sinking of *Lancastria* to the surface of our Second World War knowledge. She has, undoubtedly, brought comfort to many as they have mourned over the years, as they still mourn today – and will do in the future. As the graves, the medal and the memorial will endure, largely because of Fiona, so too will the knowledge of the tragedy. Fiona has dedicated much of her life to this cause, and as much as I would like to see the British government lift the 'D' notice and give the wreck the 'official' status she has long campaigned for, nothing can take away what she has done to ensure knowledge and remembrance of *Lancastria*.

Those who perished that day will be remembered.

★★★

Below is a poem taken from the *Lancastria* Archive, written by *Lancastria* survivor Ernest Archibald, whilst he was recovering from his injuries:

THE 17TH OF JUNE:

It was the 17th of June; the Dunkirk scene was past,
The bulk of Britain's fighting men had landed home at last,
But still there were some thousands who waited there in France,
Standing at the harbours, waiting for a chance.

The chance did come one morning, 'Twas the 17th of June,
We saw a ship come gliding near, by the early moon.
The orders then were given – Stand by! Get ready to sail!
That ship it held six thousand, packed from funnel to rail.

Each man was happy, knowing that altho' they had to run,
That ship would give another chance to beat the dirty Hun!
'Twas the 17th of June when we were out at sea,
We heard the drone of planes on high and knew who they would be!

Nearer yet they came and nearer, four planes from out the sky,
We didn't think then, that of us, four thousand were to die!
The guns were manned, we waited tense, we knew what had to come;
Then diving low, they fired at us, their bullets did get some.

Then back they came, roaring low, dropping all they had,
One by one they did the same, it was like Hell gone mad!
'Twas the 17th of June, that ship was sinking fast,
The ship that was to take us home had met her fate at last!

The lifeboats then were lowered, crammed full enough to sink!
And men with full packs on, they jumped – they had no time to think.
The sea was then a mass of men, of dead men and of dying.
And many more were drowning fast – too tired to keep on trying.

But now they sleep on the bottom deep, these men who gave their all,
They died for one and each of us, these men who answered the call.
We'll think of them as years roll by when the sea's lit up by the moon,
When they sank the proud LANCASTRIA on the 17th of June!

Ernest Archibald
(Printed with kind permission of his daughter, Mrs Jane Leiper.)

NOTES

1 Brian Crabb, *The Forgotten Tragedy: The Story of the Sinking of HMT* Lancastria, Shaun Tyas Donington, 2002
2 www.navyhistory.org/2021/09/the-lancastria-tragedy/
3 Lancastria.org.uk

CLOSING WORDS

Well, here you are, dear reader, at the end of this book. I wonder what you will take with you from these true, heartfelt memories of the Second World War. I know I have written it before. and I am sure I will write it again, but I do feel so strongly that through truth we can understand so much more about all circumstances. So, I hope, therefore, that this book achieves its core purpose: to provide a clearer understanding of what it was like for so many women who lived throughout the Second World War.

Why does this matter? Do we need to 'understand' a conflict that took place some eighty years ago? My argument would be 'yes', we do. Because, as this is written in the autumn of 2021, there is still much conflict in the world, so much division, so much needless grief and suffering. Surely, we need to draw strength from whatever resource we can; and these women show us that however hard and challenging a situation is, it can be survived. But also, I think, the message is that just surviving – getting through the day – is not enough. If something is bad, or wrong, that situation needs to be made better. During my conversations with these women (and their family members in the case of those whose stories I was given), they repeatedly expressed disappointment, frustration, and sadness at the fact that lives in many parts of the world are still being dictated, and ruined, by war. But through that message of concern was another message – that of hope. That we should never give up believing that the world can be a better place.

These women went through so much during the war, as you know now, having read their stories. The privilege of them opening their hearts and minds to me in the way they have is something I will always hold very dear; sometimes, during these conversations, I have realised just how painful it is for them to remember much of which they recalled. So why did they do it?

So that they – and the millions they represent – might not be forgotten? Yes. Absolutely. But beyond even that message of Remembrance is the message of strength and courage these women have chosen to give us.

I am trying not to be sentimental, but I can't let this book be published without sharing my own thoughts about how important I feel it is; not only for better understanding about the past, but because of what it gives us to help us manage the present, and the future. I won't make this too much longer – not least of all because this book is about our *Remarkable Women*, not me – but I would like to return to our women, and complete the picture for you as to how I came to write their stories. I want you to know them, almost as well as I do …

The first chapter I completed was Dorothy's. Dorothy lives not far from me in Suffolk; she showed much interest in my previous collection of Second World War memories, which led her, quite naturally, to tell me of her own war years. Yes, I had knowledge of child evacuation gained through read-ing books and seeing exhibitions at museums, but Dorothy's words made it real. These are the true words of a child who was sent away from home, not knowing when (or if) she would see her parents again.

Through Dorothy, I was introduced to Laurette, who gave me her mother Vera's story of being a Battle of Britain plotter. Believe me, I knew nothing of this vital hub of our history until writing this story. It was Laurette who introduced me to Ann Birch, so that I could tell her mother's story, too, about Burma.

Three stories, from one conversation. All completely different, all immensely important.

Gwen, Ena, Clarice and Lee all came to me through associations they are connected with, after I reached out to them. To remind you, Gwen is our Land Army lady, Ena is our Air Transport Auxiliary engineer[1], Clarice is our nurse and Lee is our *Kindertransport* veteran. These associations are important, which is why I want to mention them; they bring together many people, such as Gwen, Ena, Clarice and Lee, so they can share their experiences – no doubt forging last friendships, and helping them make sense, too, of what was challenging or painful in that experience. These organisations are also extremely important educational resources.

Mary Wilson is the mother of close friends of mine, also in Suffolk; the whole family love telling stories. I was so pleased when Mary agreed to reflect on her war years for me. I didn't know lady almoners existed before we spoke!

I 'found' Yoka through a Dutch family I met over twenty years ago now, during a brief (but happy!) few months living in the north of the Netherlands. I reached out to them hoping they might remember me; indeed, they did – also showing empathy for what I am trying to achieve with this book. It wasn't long before I was introduced to Yoka. I interviewed her on Zoom from her home in California, as I did Lee. I would have loved, of course, to talk to these (remarkable) women in person, but in life we have to do what we can and both these 'remote meetings' went as well as they possibly could. Technically everything worked, and I was able to talk to them in their homes – both were in their kitchens – age no barrier at all.

This brings me to Galina. This is quite a story in itself! When I began this book my eldest son (who as I write this is 14 years old) suggested I should include a story about a Russian woman who fought on the front line as part of the Red Army. How could I not agree? How could such a story not be fascinating, but also important for this book because the fact hundreds of Russian women served in the same way as men during the Second World War is still not widely known. So I was determined to write it … and a Russian voice has enabled me to the tell the wider story of the country that lost more of its people than any other country in the world. So, I 'hunted' long and hard for a Russian voice. I contacted the Russian embassy in London, and our reciprocal embassy in Moscow. I emailed authors who have written on this subject – mostly in America – and sent messages to museums, in America and Russia. No response from anyone. I don't give up easily, as you may have gathered, but I was starting to try to tell myself that it wasn't the 'end of the world' not to have a Russian chapter … but I then suddenly remembered another friend who lived in Russia and who, importantly too, still cares very much about it. He approached a friend of his who still lives in Moscow, and within days I was introduced to Galina, Russia's last surviving female Second World War aviator.

I read through some Russian newspaper cuttings about Galina (roughly translated into broken English) and did as much research as I could before 'interviewing' Galina myself, through a (very excited) Russian translator, on Zoom. It is hard interviewing someone when you don't know what they are saying, but Galina, and the translator, could not have been more helpful; it was a thoroughly enjoyable Zoom that I shall long remember. The text has since gone backwards and forwards several times – as it should – and Galina seems very pleased her story is being told for this book; but most of all it is, as she says, for the millions of Russians who died during the Second World War.

Now to Anka, to whom I was introduced by a Croatian friend, Tamara, from my BBC News days (some years ago now!). Whilst I thought about the chapters I particularly wanted for this book, I felt a chapter about the Partisans in Yugoslavia was very important – not only because it is so complex and therefore fascinating, but also because this part of the world has a special place in my heart. I will just take a moment to explain why …

Tamara reminded me one day of the appalling massacre in Srebrenica in 1995, during which some 8,000 Muslim Bosnian boys and their fathers were marched into the hills and shot by Bosnian Serb forces. I knew about this when it happened, of course, because it was in the news, but hearing Tamara talk about it compelled me to want to visit … and because my time at the BBC coincided with the tenth anniversary of this dreadful massacre, I suggested to the head of news it should be remembered; thankfully that was agreed, and I visited with a camera crew to recall the memory.

Whilst I was there, I was taken to the hills where some of the atrocities took place; I walked amongst the hundreds of small, green gravestones that stretch as far as the eye can see in graveyards, one for each of the boys and men so cruelly taken. I also met a lady who was involved in a project to extract DNA (for identification purposes) from the bones of many of the skeletons that litter the area - and I met mothers, wives and sisters left behind. These women may have been ten years into their grief when I met them, but no time will heal their suffering. They were gentle, unassuming, glad to talk, all of them welcoming; and none let me leave their home without giving me a gift – my favourite one of all was a crocheted light-blue halter-neck top, which I still wear.

Many of these grieving women would, I am sure, have been daughters, granddaughters and nieces of wartime Partisan supporters like Anka. The strength the Partisan women needed, and found they had, during the war changed their society irrevocably after 1945; doors opened and opportunities prevailed that, before, would only have been for the men. However, equally important is the message of equality that prevailed: the Partisan women, thousands of them, left their society without a shadow of doubt that women should not be underestimated. The women I met in Srebrenica were heart-broken, but they were not defeated. I am sure they had Partisan blood …

Finally, Midori and Fiona. I have known Fiona now for over six years; I came to know her, initially, because of her care for remembrance of *Lancastria*, as told in her epilogue. I didn't know about this disaster, this appalling sinking of a troopship in June 1940 which resulted in so much life lost, until I read about it in my grandfather's Second World War diary, the writing up of which began my own personal journey of becoming an author of so many more memories. His memoir (*Six Weeks of Blenheim Summer*, about his time as an RAF pilot during the Battle of France in 1940) is now published.[2] My Uncle David wrote a note of introduction to that book, writing that if his father 'knew his story was being published he would want it to be dedicated to those who lost their lives on *Lancastria*'. After discovering the enormous scale of loss and pain as a result of the bombing of *Lancastria* and reading about Fiona's impassioned search for justice, I contacted her and helped her with her campaign. Fiona's story reminds us of those who died in the war who do not even have a grave. Might this book lead, at last, to her questions being answered?[3]

And through Fiona I was introduced, very thankfully, to Midori. I had been looking for a Japanese voice as hard as I had looked for our Russian voice. Again, I had contacted museums, the embassy and authors, to no avail. So, imagine how pleased I was when Fiona told me, during the course of one of our conversations about *Lancastria*, about her Japanese friend Harumi, whose mother (Midori, almost 90 years old) is alive and well and living in Japan; would I like to be introduced?

That brings me to the end of my summary about all of our *Remarkable Women*; I think remarkable is an absolutely fine word to use because of their survival during the war, the way they have lived their lives since, and the fact they have told their stories, but – and I hope they won't mind me saying this – they are actually 'ordinary' women, too. There is nothing wrong with being an 'ordinary' woman. They know they are the voices behind millions of others who coped, struggled, got exhausted, angry, frustrated, and were frightened as they were. It comforts me, when thinking about some of their saddest, most painful times, to remember some of the most touching images revealed in their stories: Yoka's cyclamen, Sha's 'buns' in Midori's story, the milk Dorothy gave to the kittens, Ena's friend singing whilst sitting on the wing of an aircraft in their hangar, Gwen hiding in a shed because Italian prisoners-of-war were teasing her with love songs, and the 'single rose that defiantly poked its head through a pile of rubble, standing on a long stalk like a sentinel over the devastation' in Clarice's story.

Just before I finish, I am reminded of another 'remarkable' woman: Mady Gerrard, whose memory is in my previous book of war memories[4] *Remarkable Journeys of the Second World War* (this one is written as its 'companion' book, or sequel).

Mady was a Holocaust survivor. As a young teenager she experienced both the Bergen-Belsen and Auschwitz concentration camps; her memory is laid bare in *Remarkable Journeys*. However, what is poignant for this book too, and why I am recalling it, are the words of John Randall who liberated Mady, and with whom she had a chance (and wonderful) reunion seventy years later. Both John Randall and Mady have now died, but his words describing why the Holocaust must be remembered will endure. Holocaust crimes were, without a doubt, some of the most awful inflicted during the Second World War years, but there was so much appalling suffering, across the world. I think he speaks for all with the following words from the foreword to Mady's own self-published book, *Full Circle*:[5]

The attempted annihilation of the Jewish people and the manner of its execution must always remain one of the greatest and most disgraceful crimes in history. The thousands of brilliantly talented people from all aspects of our lives – art, literature, medicine, music, philosophy – and every walk of life is so awful that its magnitude can never be exaggerated.

In spite of the horrors the survivors have a history of extraordinary bravery, a determination to survive and the indomitable spirit to never give up hope. This must be an inspiration to all of us.

With the war over but still no security living in an ugly world still full of hate and depravity – there is still hope and determination to survive. My final sobering fear is that these crimes are already happening again, and we must resolve to fight this situation as vigorously as we can.

This is a poignant but important message to leave you with. War, leading to the deliberate human infliction of pain on other humans, is simply as appalling as it is wrong. Because of the suffering of so much in the past, let us all try to learn for humanity today and in the future.

Victoria

NOTES

1. www.womenslandarmy.co.uk; www.airtransportaux.org.uk; www.waafassociation. co.uk; www.kindertransport.org
2. Alastair Panton DFC, OBE, CB and Victoria Panton Bacon, *Six Weeks of Blenheim Summer*, Penguin, 2018
3. Victoria Panton Bacon, *Remarkable Journeys of the Second World War*, History Press, 2020
4. Mady Gerrard, *Full Circle*, Duncan Print Group, 2006

ACKNOWLEDGEMENTS

Firstly, thank you always and so very much to all the Remarkable Women whose memories fill the pages of this book: Dorothy Drew, Ena Botting, Vera Saies, Clarice Jacques, Gwen Raggett, Mary Wilson, Yoka Verdoner, Midori Yamazaki, Mollie Birch, Lee Edwards, Galina Beltsova, Anka Alucevic and Fiona Symon. My gratitude is for all of them – whether they are still alive today, or no longer with us. However, thanking them for their stories is just a part of what we must be grateful for – it is their service during the Second World War for which we owe the greatest debt of gratitude.

And, whilst we thank them, we must think too of the thousands – millions – of women across the world who served, cared, fought, travelled and lived alongside them. These memories are for all of them.

I could not have written any of these chapters without support, and help, from friends and family members of all our Remarkable Women, and those who represent the many organisations and associations I have reached out to. Thank you all, especially:

The British chapters: Geoff Botting and John Webster of the Air Transport Auxiliary Association; Laurette and Cedric Burton and the staff at the Battle of Britain Bunker in Uxbridge; Rosie Ives, Marian Cope of the Women's Auxiliary Air Force Association and Bob Sanderson of the Princess Mary's Royal Air Force Nursing Service; Heather Raggett and Cherish and Skye Watton of the Women's Land Army Association; Alastair and Suzy Wilson and Sarah Hawker.

The global chapters: Barend ter Haar, Vera ter Haar-van Oyen, Louise ter Haar, Dik van der Meulen, Eline Hopperus Buma and Pieter 't Hart; Harumi Currie; Ann Birch; Tony Harris, Lena Carlebach and the Kindertransport Association; Nick Jenkins, Rupert Wilbraham, Dmitry Levin, Tatiana Beltsova, Irina Sivkova, Galina Mamontova, Bruce and Nina Gardner; Ranko Alujevic, Tvrtko Jakovina and Tamara Kovacevic.

Thank you, too, to Emma Shercliff – my agent – for her attentiveness, encouragement and positivity! And also to Amy Rigg, Jezz Palmer, Martin Latham, Jemma Cox and Cynthia Hamilton at The History Press for helping me bring these stories to fruition; and to my own family and friends for being patient with me, listening to me read draft chapters and allowing me to share my excitement about many of the revelations as I have discovered them. In no particular order, special thanks to: William Drew-Batty, my children Rollo and Ranulph, Richard Bacon, and my brother Henry.

Thank you, too, to Professor Christopher Hand for his careful and attentive proofreading.

Thank you, too, to Miriam Frank, Lucinda Hawksley, Pat Rorke and Wendy Holden for your endorsements. Miriam and Pat, your support for this book means so much to me; your own Second World War experience gives you a special understanding and empathy. Thank you for your words.

Thank you very much too to Rt Hon Penny Mordaunt MP for the thoughtful foreword, for which I am hugely grateful.

Fiona's epilogue is a remembrance chapter. Fiona has asked that the people listed overleaf are mentioned, because without them Fiona wouldn't have been able to do what she has done to remember those who died on the *Lancastria*, in June 1940.

Above all, these memories have been given so we remember.

Thank you all,

Victoria

P.S. Thank you William, too, for your music.

EPILOGUE THANKS, IN THE WORDS OF FIONA SYMON

All my love to my wonderful, patient and supportive husband Ian whose encouragement set me on the *Lancastria* road;

Those who served on the *Lancastria* Association of Scotland committee to whom is owed so much for their unstinting work;

The author of *The Forgotten Tragedy*, Mr Brian J. Crabb, whose unfailing help with information was so much appreciated. He has become a dear friend;

Mr Mark Hirst – co-founder of the association with me and who, with MSP Christine Grahame did amazing work for the *Lancastria* Commemorative Medal;

Ld Lt Jill Young and D Ld Lt Gill Aitkenhead for their incredible support at Clydebank;

Fife sculptor Marion Smith who did such careful research which resulted in the beautiful *Lancastria* memorial at Clydebank;

Mr Brian Dean who gifted the wonderful model of the ship which is in a case built and donated by Babcock International who also made the story-boards telling the ship's life;

Lastly, the many, many people who contributed to all the remembrance services over the years. Thank you all. None of the achievements would have been possible without the great *Lancastria* family of helpers.

BIBLIOGRAPHY

PUBLISHED BOOKS

Alexeivich, Svetlana, *The Unwomanly Face of War*, Penguin Classics, 2017

Bishop, Patrick, *Bomber Boys, 'Fighting Back 1940–45'*, Harper Perennial, 2008

de Zwarte, Ingrid, *De Hongerwinter*, Prometheus, 2019

Ellis, Mary and Melody Foreman, *A Spitfire Girl: The World's Greatest Female Ferry Pilot Tells Her Story*, Frontline books, 2016

Frank, Miriam, *My Innocent Absence*, Arcadia Books, 2010

Goodpaster Strebe, Amy, *Flying For Her Country: The American and Soviet Women Military Pilots of World War II*, Potomac Books Inc, 2009

Gunston, Bill, *Aircraft of World War II*, Octopus Books Ltd, 1980

Holden, Wendy, *Born Survivors*, Sphere, 2015

Holland, James, *The Battle of Britain*, Penguin Random House, 2017

Iredale, Will, *The Kamakazi Hunters: Fighting for the War in the Pacific, 1945*, Macmillan, 2015

Noggle, Anne, *A Dance with Death: Soviet Airwomen in World War II*, Texas A&M University Press, 1994

Panton Bacon, Victoria, *Remarkable Journeys of the Second World War*, The History Press, 2020

Panton, Alastair and Victoria Panton Bacon, *Six Weeks of Blenheim Summer*, Penguin Random House, 2018

Pearson, Simon and Ed Gorman, *Battle of Britain*, Hodder and Stoughton, 2020

Purnell's History of the Second World War, Phoebus Publishing Ltd, *c*. 1970.

Randall, John and M.J. Trow, *The Last Gentleman of the SAS*, Penguin Random House, 2014

Saywell, Shelley, *Women in War*, Viking Penguin Inc., 1985

Verdoner, Yoka, and Francisca Verdoner-Kan, eds, *Signs of Life: The Letters of Hilde Verdoner-Sluizer*, Acropolis Books Ltd, 1990

SELF-PUBLISHED BOOKS

Jacques, Clarice, *Travels with a Gasmask 1939–1945*, privately printed by Flexpress, Leicester, 2020

Rorke, Patricia, *Every Common Bush*, privately printed by CPI AntonyRowe, Eastbourne, 2007

Gerrard, Mady, *Full Circle*, privately printed by Duncan Print Group Ltd, Welwyn Garden City, 2006

NEWSPAPERS

Daily Mail, 19 August 1978
The Guardian, 18 June 2018
Jutarnji (Croatia), 2 October 2021

ONLINE SOURCES

airforcemag.com
airpowerasia.com
airvectors.net
annefrank.org/en/anne-frank/go-in-depth/why-did-hitler-hate-jews
atamuseum.org
baesystems.com/en/heritage/vickers-wellington
bbc.co.uk/ahistoryoftheworld
bbcnews.co.uk
britannica.com
carrotmuseum.co.uk
factfile.org/10-facts-about-anderson-shelter
forces.net/news
hharp.org/library/gosh/general/hospital-almoner
holland.com/global/tourism
iwm.org.uk/history
kindertransport.org
nationalww2museum.org
pmrafnsassociation.co.uk
rafmuseum.org.uk/research/online-exhibitions/women-of-the-air-force
smithsonianmag.com/history
the-past.com
ushmm.org (United States Holocaust Memorial Museum)
warfarehistorynetwork.com/2019/01/11/incomplete-victory-at-malaise
wartimememoriesproject.com/ww2/airfields/airfield
womenslandarmy.co.uk
wondersofworldaviation.com/bristol_pegasus

The History Press
The destination for history
www.thehistorypress.co.uk